DATE DUE

DEC 1 2 2007	
JUL 2 8 2010	
NOV 3 0 2010	
JUN 2 5 2012	
Dec. 5, 2012	
NOV 2 8 2016	

BRODART, CO.   Cat. No. 23-221-003

DOVER · THRIFT · EDITIONS

Great Speeches by African Americans

Frederick Douglass, Sojourner Truth, Dr. Martin Luther King, Jr., Barack Obama, and Others

Edited by

JAMES DALEY

DOVER PUBLICATIONS, INC.
Mineola, New York

DOVER THRIFT EDITIONS

GENERAL EDITOR: MARY CAROLYN WALDREP
EDITOR OF THIS VOLUME: JANET BAINE KOPITO

Acknowledgments

"What Does American Democracy Mean to Me?" by Mary McLeod Bethune, reprinted with permission of Mary McLeod Bethune Foundation, Bethune-Cookman College, Daytona Beach, Florida.

"I Have a Dream" by Martin Luther King, Jr., reprinted by arrangement with the Estate of Martin Luther King Jr., c/o Writers House as agent for the proprietor, New York, NY. *Copyright 1963 Martin Luther King Jr., copyright renewed 1991 Coretta Scott King.*

"The Ballot or The Bullet" by Malcolm X. TM 2005 Malcolm X by CMG Worldwide, Inc. www.CMGWorldwide.com

"The Black Woman in Contemporary America" by Shirley Chisholm, reprinted by arrangement with the Estate of Shirley Chisholm.

"The Constitution: A Living Document" by Thurgood Marshall, from the Howard Law Journal (Volume 30, Issue 4), reprinted with the permission of the Howard Law Journal.

"Knox College Commencement Address" by Senator Barack Obama, reprinted with the permission of Barack Obama.

Copyright

Bibliographical Note

Great Speeches by African Americans: Frederick Douglass, Sojourner Truth, Dr. Martin Luther King, Jr., Barack Obama, and Others is a new compilation, first published by Dover Publications, Inc., in 2006. An Introduction has been written specially for the present edition by James Daley, who has also provided a biographical note for the author of each speech. For the sake of authenticity, inconsistencies in capitalization and hyphenation occasionally have been retained in the texts of the present edition.

Library of Congress Cataloging-in-Publication Data

Great Speeches by African Americans : Frederick Douglass, Sojourner Truth, Dr. Martin Luther King, Jr., Barack Obama, and others / edited by James Daley.
    p. cm. — (Dover thrift editions)
    ISBN 0-486-44761-8 (pbk.)
    1. Speeches, addresses, etc., American—African American authors. 2. African Americans—History—Sources. 3. African American orators. I. Daley, James. II. Series.

PS663.N4G74 2006
815.008'0896073—dc22
                                                        2005046627

Manufactured in the United States of America
Dover Publications, Inc., 31 East 2nd Street, Mineola, N.Y. 11501

Introduction to the Dover Edition

> "Democracy is for me, and for 12 million black Americans,
> a goal towards which our nation is marching."

THUS BEGINS Mary McLeod Bethune's historic speech, "What Does American Democracy Mean to Me?," in which she states with the utmost clarity that even in 1939—seventy-one years after the ratification of the Fourteenth Amendment, which granted citizenship to all former slaves—true democracy lay still further in the future of our great nation.

Bethune goes on to speak of the "measure" of democracy that had been extended to African Americans, and how, for example, it both afforded theretofore impossible rates of literacy, while nonetheless withholding all but a fraction of the educational opportunities granted to white Americans. In short, her speech spoke of the struggle—long fought and far from over—of which she intuitively knew our country had yet to see the heights. As Bethune prophetically states in the final paragraph of her speech, "Perhaps the greatest battle is before us, the fight for a new America: fearless, free, united, morally re-armed, in which 12 million Negroes, shoulder to shoulder with their fellow Americans, will strive that this nation under God will have a new birth of freedom, and that the government of the people, for the people and by the people shall not perish from the earth."

It is in keeping with Bethune's conception of American democracy that this anthology has been prepared. By beginning at a time when slavery was legal and commonplace, and ending in the present (though, of course, still looking forward), this volume attempts to show, using the voices of our country's greatest and most influential African Americans, how the goal of democracy has been fought for, dreamed of, and brought within our reach.

With the speeches of Henry Highland Garnet, Jermain Wesley Loguen, Sojourner Truth, Frederick Douglass, and John Sweat Rock, we glimpse the decades leading up to the issuance of the Emancipation

Proclamation (1862). These speeches reflect the horrors of their day, speaking out against such atrocities as the Fugitive Slave Law, while calling to action black and white alike to overthrow the system and abolish slavery forever.

The speeches that were presented in the eight decades after the Civil War include the voices of Booker T. Washington, Mary Church Terrell, W. E. B. Du Bois, Marcus Garvey, and Mary McLeod Bethune, among many others. These brilliant orations trace the country's movement from the twilight of slavery to the dawn of the modern civil rights movement. Touching upon issues such as suffrage, lynching, education, sexism, prejudice, and poverty, they vividly illustrate the nation's struggle to cope with the legacy of slavery, and to set the stage for a new generation of activism and change.

Comprising the examples of the modern age's struggle towards democracy are Martin Luther King Jr.'s iconic speech, "I Have a Dream," and Malcolm X's seething polemic, "The Ballot or the Bullet," as well as stirring speeches by two groundbreaking public figures: Shirley Chisholm, the first African-American U.S. congresswoman, and Thurgood Marshall, the first African-American U.S. Supreme Court justice.

Finally, representative of the twenty-first century is Barack Obama, the honorable senator from Illinois—already a legendary orator in his own right. In his commencement address to the Knox College class of 2005, after speaking of how Abraham Lincoln upheld the great principles of equality and freedom, he presents his own views on the attainment of the goal of democracy:

> My hope for all of you is that as you leave here today, you decide to keep these principles alive in your own life and in the life of this country. You will be tested. You won't always succeed. But know that you have it within your power to try. That generations who have come before you faced these same fears and uncertainties in their own time. And that through our collective labor, and through God's providence, and our willingness to shoulder each other's burdens, America will continue on its precious journey towards that distant horizon, and a better day.

James Daley
Editor

Contents

Great Speeches
by African Americans

Henry Highland Garnet

(1815–1882)

AN ADDRESS TO THE SLAVES OF THE UNITED STATES OF AMERICA
August 16, 1843

Born into slavery, Henry Highland Garnet escaped from Maryland to New York in 1824, where he pursued his education at the African Free School No. 1 and the Oneida Institute; he eventually became an ordained Presbyterian minister. Garnet delivered the following speech at the National Convention of Negro Citizens in Buffalo, New York.

BRETHREN AND FELLOW CITIZENS: Your brethren of the North, East, and West have been accustomed to meet together in national conventions, to sympathize with each other, and to weep over your unhappy condition. In these meetings we have addressed all classes of the free, but we have never, until this time, sent a word of consolation and advice to you. We have been contented in sitting still and mourning over your sorrows, earnestly hoping that before this day your sacred Liberties would have been restored. But we have hoped in vain. Years have rolled on, and tens of thousands have been borne on streams of blood and tears to the shores of eternity. While you have been oppressed, we have also been partakers with you; nor can we be free while you are enslaved. We, therefore, write to you as being bound with you.

Many of you are bound to us, not only by the ties of a common humanity, but we are connected by the more tender relations of parents, wives, husbands, children, brothers, and sisters, and friends. As such we most affectionately address you.

Slavery has fixed a deep gulf between you and us, and while it shuts out from you the relief and consolation which your friends would willingly render, it afflicts and persecutes you with a fierceness which we

1

might not expect to see in the fiends of hell. But still the Almighty Father of mercies has left to us a glimmering ray of hope, which shines out like a lone star in a cloudy sky. Mankind are becoming wiser, and better—the oppressor's power is fading, and you every day are becoming better informed and more numerous. Your grievances, brethren, are many. We shall not attempt in this short address to present to the world all the dark catalogue of this nation's sins which have been committed upon an innocent people. Nor is it indeed necessary, for you feel them from day to day, and all the civilized world looks upon them with amazement.

Two hundred and twenty-seven years ago the first of our injured race were brought to the shores of America. They came not with glad spirits to select their homes in the New World. They came not with their own consent, to find an unmolested enjoyment of the blessings of this fruitful soil. The first dealings they had with men calling themselves Christians exhibited to them the worst features of corrupt and sordid hearts, and convinced them that no cruelty is too great, no villainy and no robbery too abhorrent for even enlightened men to perform, when influenced by avarice and lust. Neither did they come flying upon the wings of Liberty to a land of freedom. But they came with broken hearts from their beloved native land and were doomed to unrequited toil and deep degradation. Nor did the evil of their bondage end at their emancipation by death. Succeeding generations inherited their chains, and millions have come from eternity into time, and have returned again to the world of spirits, cursed and ruined by American Slavery.

The propagators of the system, or their immediate successors, very soon discovered its growing evil and its tremendous wickedness, and secret promises were made to destroy it. The gross inconsistency of a people holding slaves, who had themselves "ferried o'er the wave" for freedom's sake, was too apparent to be entirely overlooked. The voice of Freedom cried, "Emancipate your slaves." Humanity supplicated with tears for the deliverance of the children of Africa. Wisdom urged her solemn plea. The bleeding captive pleaded his innocence and pointed to Christianity who stood weeping at the cross. Jehovah frowned upon the nefarious institution, and thunderbolts, red with vengeance, struggled to leap forth to blast the guilty wretches who maintained it. But all was vain. Slavery had stretched its dark wings of death over the land, the Church stood silently by, the priests prophesied falsely, and the people loved to have it so. Its throne is established, and now it reigns triumphantly.

Nearly three millions of your fellow citizens are prohibited by law and public opinion (which in this country is stronger than law) from reading the Book of Life. Your intellect has been destroyed as much as possible, and every ray of light they have attempted to shut out from your minds. The oppressors themselves have become involved in the ruin. They have become weak, sensual, and rapacious; they have cursed you; they have cursed themselves; they have cursed the earth which they have trod.

The colonies threw the blame upon England. They said that the mother country entailed the evil upon them, and that they would rid themselves of it if they could. The world thought they were sincere, and the philanthropic pitied them. But time soon tested their sincerity. In a few years the colonists grew strong and severed themselves from the British government. Their independence was declared, and they took their station among the sovereign powers of the earth. The declaration was a glorious document. Sages admired it, and the patriotic of every nation reverenced the Godlike sentiments which it contained. When the power of government returned to their hands, did they emancipate the slaves? No; they rather added new links to our chains. Were they ignorant of the principles of Liberty? Certainly they were not. The sentiments of their revolutionary orators fell in burning eloquence upon their hearts, and with one voice they cried, "Liberty or death." Oh, what a sentence was that! It ran from soul to soul like electric fire and nerved the arms of thousands to fight in the holy cause of Freedom. Among the diversity of opinions that are entertained in regard to physical resistance, there are but a few found to gainsay that stern declaration. We are among those who do not.

Slavery! How much misery is comprehended in that single word. What mind is there that does not shrink from its direful effects? Unless the image of God be obliterated from the soul, all men cherish the love of Liberty. The nice discerning political economist does not regard the sacred right more than the untutored African who roams in the wilds of Congo. Nor has the one more right to the full enjoyment of his freedom than the other. In everyman's mind the good seeds of Liberty are planted, and he who brings his fellow down so low as to make him contented with a condition of slavery commits the highest crime against God and man. Brethren, your oppressors aim to do this. They endeavor to make you as much like brutes as possible. When they have blinded the eyes of your mind; when they have embittered the sweet waters of life; when they have shut out the light which shines from the word of God—then, and not till then, has American slavery done its perfect work.

To such degradation it is sinful in the extreme for you to make voluntary submission. The divine commandments you are in duty bound to reverence and obey. If you do not obey them, you will surely meet with the displeasure of the Almighty. He requires you to love Him supremely, and your neighbor as yourself, to keep the Sabbath day holy, to search the Scriptures, and bring up your children with respect for His laws, and to worship no other God but Him. But slavery sets all these at nought, and hurls defiance in the face of Jehovah. The forlorn condition in which you are placed does not destroy your moral obligation to God. You are not certain of Heaven, because you suffer yourselves to remain in a state of slavery, where you cannot obey the commandments of the Sovereign of the universe. If the ignorance of slavery is a passport to Heaven, then it is a blessing, and no curse, and you should rather desire its perpetuity than its abolition. God will not receive slavery, nor ignorance, nor any other state of mind, for love and obedience to Him. Your condition does not absolve you from your moral obligation. The diabolical injustice by which your liberties are cloven down, neither God nor angels, nor just men command you to suffer for a single moment. Therefore it is your solemn and imperative duty to use every means, both moral, intellectual and physical, that promises success. If a band of heathen men should attempt to enslave a race of Christians, and to place their children under the influence of some false religion, surely Heaven would frown upon the men who would not resist such aggression, even to death. If, on the other hand, a band of Christians should attempt to enslave a race of heathen men, and to entail slavery upon them, and to keep them in heathenism in the midst of Christianity, the God of Heaven would smile upon every effort which the injured might make to disenthrall themselves.

Brethren, it is as wrong for your lordly oppressors to keep you in slavery as it was for the man thief to steal our ancestors from the coast of Africa. You should therefore now use the same manner of resistance as would have been just in our ancestors when the bloody footprints of the first remorseless soul thief was placed upon the shores of our fatherland. The humblest peasant is as free in the sight of God as the proudest monarch that ever swayed a scepter. Liberty is a spirit sent out from God and, like its great Author, is no respecter of persons.

Brethren, the time has come when you must act for yourselves. It is an old and true saying that, "if hereditary bondsmen would be free, they must themselves strike the blow." You can plead your own cause and do the work of emancipation better than any others. The nations of the Old World are moving in the great cause of universal freedom, and some of them at least will, ere long, do you justice. The combined powers of Europe have placed their broad seal of disapprobation upon the African slave trade. But in the slaveholding parts of the United States the trade is as brisk as ever. They buy and sell you as though you were brute beasts. The North has done much; her opinion of slavery in the abstract is known. But in regard to the South, we adopt the opinion of the *New York Evangelist*—"We have advanced so far, that the cause apparently waits for a more effectual door to be thrown open than has been yet." We are about to point you to that more effectual door. Look around you and behold the bosoms of your loving wives heaving with untold agonies! Hear the cries of your poor children! Remember the stripes your fathers bore. Think of the torture and disgrace of your noble mothers. Think of your wretched sisters, loving virtue and purity, as they are driven into concubinage and are exposed to the unbridled lusts of incarnate devils. Think of the undying glory that hangs around the ancient name of Africa—and forget not that you are native-born American citizens, and as such you are justly entitled to all the rights that are granted to the freest. Think how many tears you have poured out upon the soil which you have cultivated with unrequited toil and enriched with your blood; and then go to your lordly enslavers and tell them plainly that you *are determined to be free*. Appeal to their sense of justice and tell them that they have no more right to oppress you than you have to enslave them. Entreat them to remove the grievous burdens which they have imposed upon you, and to remunerate you for your labor. Promise them renewed diligence in the cultivation of the soil, if they will render to you an equivalent for your services. Point them to the increase of happiness and prosperity in the British West Indies since the Act of Emancipation. Tell them, in language which they cannot misunderstand, of the exceeding sinfulness of slavery and of a future judgement and of the righteous retributions of an indignant God. Inform them that all you desire is freedom, and that nothing else will suffice. Do this, and forever after cease to toil for the heartless tyrants, who give you no other reward but stripes and abuse. If they then commence the work of death, they, and not you, will be responsible for the consequences. You had far better all die—*die immediately*—than live slaves and entail your wretchedness upon your posterity. If you would be free in this generation, here is your only hope. However much you and all of us may desire it, there is not much hope of redemption without the shedding of blood. If you must bleed, let it all come at once—rather *die freemen than live to be slaves.* It is impossible, like the children of Israel, to make a grand exodus from the land of bondage. The Pharaohs are on both sides of the blood-red waters! You cannot move *en masse,* to the dominions of the British Queen, nor can you pass through Florida and overrun Texas and at last find peace in Mexico. The propagators of American slavery are spending their blood and treasure that they may plant the black flag in the heart of Mexico and riot in the halls of the Montezumas. In the language of the Reverend Robert Hall, when addressing the volunteers of Bristol who were rushing forth to repel the invasion of Napoleon, who threatened to lay waste the fair homes of England, "Religion is too much interested in your behalf not to shed over you her most gracious influences."

You will not be compelled to spend much time in order to become inured to hardships. From the first moment that you breathed the air of heaven, you have been accustomed to nothing else but hardships. The heroes of the American Revolution were never put upon harder fare than a peck of corn and a few herrings per week. You have not become enervated by the luxuries of life. Your sternest energies have been beaten out upon the anvil of severe trial. Slavery has done this to make you subservient to its own purposes. But it has done more than this; it has prepared you for any emergency. If you receive good treatment, it is what you could hardly expect; if you meet with pain, sorrow, and even death, these are the common lot of the slaves.

Fellow men, patient sufferers, behold your dearest rights crushed to the earth! See your sons murdered, and your wives, mothers and sisters doomed to prostitution. In the name of the merciful God, and by all that life is worth, let it no longer be a debatable question, whether it is better to choose liberty or death.

In 1822, Denmark Veazie, of South Carolina, formed a plan for the liberation of his fellow men. In the whole history of human efforts to overthrow slavery, a more complicated and tremendous plan was never formed. He was betrayed by the treachery of his own people, and died a martyr to freedom. Many a brave hero fell, but history, faithful to her high trust, will transcribe his name on the same monument with Moses, Hampden, Tell, Bruce and Wallace, Toussaint L'Ouverture, Lafayette and Washington. That tremendous movement shook the whole empire of slavery. The guilty soul thieves were overwhelmed with fear. It is a matter of fact that at this time, and in consequence of the threatened revolution, the slave states talked strongly of emancipation. But they blew but one blast of the trumpet of freedom, and then laid it aside. As these men became quiet, the slaveholders ceased to talk about emancipation; and now behold your condition to-day! Angels sigh over it, and humanity has long since exhausted her tears in weeping on your account!

The patriotic Nathaniel Turner followed Denmark Veazie. He was goaded to desperation by wrong and injustice. By despotism, his name has been recorded on the list of infamy, but future generations will remember him among the noble and brave.

Next arose the immortal Joseph Cinque, the hero of the *Amistad*. He was a native African, and by the help of God he emancipated a whole ship-load of his fellow men on the high seas. And he now sings of Liberty on the sunny hills of Africa and beneath his native palm trees, where he hears the lion roar and feels himself as free as that king of the forest.

Next arose Madison Washington, that bright star of freedom, and took his station in the constellation of true heroism. He was a slave on board the brig *Creole,* of Richmond, bound to New Orleans, that great slave mart, with a hundred and four others. Nineteen struck for Liberty or death. But one life was taken, and the whole were emancipated, and the vessel was carried into Nassau, New Providence.

Noble men! Those who have fallen in freedom's conflict, their memories will be cherished by the true-hearted and the God-fearing in all future generations; those who are living, their names are surrounded by a halo of glory.

Brethren, arise, arise! Strike for your lives and liberties. Now is the day and the hour. Let every slave throughout the land do this, and the days of slavery are numbered. You cannot be more oppressed than you have been; you cannot suffer greater cruelties than you have already. *Rather die freemen than live to be slaves.* Remember that you are three *millions!*

It is in your power so to torment the God-cursed slaveholders that they will be glad to let you go free. If the scale was turned, and black men were the masters and white men the slaves, every destructive agent and element would be employed to lay the oppressor low. Danger and death would meet with plagues more terrible than those of Pharaoh. But you are a patient people. You act as though you were made for the special use of these devils. You act as though your daughters were born to pamper the lusts of your masters and overseers. And worse than all, you tamely submit while your lords tear your wives from your embraces and defile them before your eyes. In the name of God, we ask, are you men? Where is the blood of your fathers? Has it all run out of your veins? Awake, awake; millions of voices are calling you! Your dead fathers speak to you from their graves. Heaven, as with a voice of thunder, calls on you to arise from the dust.

Let your motto be Resistance! *Resistance!* RESISTANCE! No oppressed people have ever secured their Liberty without resistance. What kind of resistance you had better make you must decide by the circumstances that surround you, and according to the suggestion of expediency. Brethren, adieu! Trust in the living God. Labor for the peace of the human race, and remember that you are three millions!

Jermain Wesley Loguen

(1813–1872)

I AM A FUGITIVE SLAVE
October 4, 1850

Jermain Wesley Loguen, noted clergyman and abolitionist, was born into slavery in Tennessee in 1813. Escaping first to Ontario, Canada, he settled in Rochester, New York, after attending the Oneida Institute. The following speech was delivered at City Hall in Syracuse, New York, at a meeting concerning the recently passed Fugitive Slave Act, legislation providing for the seizure and return of runaway slaves who had escaped from one state into another. In this speech, Loguen calls for the city of Syracuse to declare itself a refuge for freed slaves, a proposal that later passed by a vote of 395 to 96.

I WAS A SLAVE; I knew the dangers I was exposed to. I had made up my mind as to the course I was to take. On that score I needed no counsel, nor did the colored citizens generally. They had taken their stand—they would not be taken back to slavery. If to shoot down their assailants should forfeit their lives, such result was the least of the evil. They will have their liberties or die in their defense. What is life to me if I am to be a slave in Tennessee? My neighbors! I have lived with you many years, and you know me. My home is here, and my children were born here. I am bound to Syracuse by pecuniary interests, and social and family bonds. And do you think I can be taken away from you and from my wife and children, and be a slave in Tennessee? Has the President and his Secretary sent this enactment up here, to you, Mr. Chairman, to enforce on me in Syracuse?—and will you obey him? Did I think so meanly of you—did I suppose the people of Syracuse, strong as they are in numbers and love of liberty—or did I believe their love of liberty was so selfish, unmanly and unchristian—did I believe them so sunken and servile and degraded as to remain at their homes and labors, or, with none of that spirit which smites a tyrant down, to surround a United States Marshal to see me torn from my home and family, and hurled back to bondage— I say did I think so meanly of you, I could never come to live with you. Nor should I have stopped, on my return from Troy, twenty-four hours since, but to take my family and movables to a neighborhood which would take fire, and arms, too, to resist the least attempt to execute this diabolical law among them. Some kind and good friends advise me to quit my country, and stay in Canada, until this tempest is passed. I doubt not the sincerity of such counsellors. But my conviction is strong, that their advice comes from a lack of knowledge of themselves and the case in hand. I believe that their own bosoms are charged to the brim with qualities that will smite to the earth the villains who may interfere to enslave any man in Syracuse. I apprehend the advice is suggested by the perturbation of the moment, and not by the tranquil spirit that rules above the storm, in the eternal home of truth and wisdom. Therefore I have hesitated to adopt this advice, at least until I have the opinion of this meeting. Those friends have not canvassed this subject. I have. They are called suddenly to look at it. I have looked at it steadily, calmly, resolutely, and at length defiantly, for a long time. I tell you the people of Syracuse and of the whole North must meet this tyranny and crush it by force, or be crushed by it. This hellish enactment has precipitated the conclusion that white men must live in dishonorable submission, and colored men be slaves, or they must give their physical as well as intellectual powers to the defense of human rights. The time has come to change the tones of submission into tones of defiance,—and to tell Mr. Fillmore and Mr. Webster, if they propose to execute this measure upon us, to send on their bloodhounds. Mr. President, long ago I was beset by over-prudent and good men and women to purchase my freedom. Nay, I was frequently importuned to consent that they purchase it, and present it as evidence of their partiality to my person and character. Generous and kind as those friends were, my heart recoiled from the proposal. I owe my freedom to the God who made me, and who stirred me to claim it against all other beings in God's universe. I will not, nor will I consent, that anybody else shall countenance the claims of a vulgar despot to my soul and body. Were I in chains, and did these kind people come to buy me out of prison, I would acknowledge the boon with inexpressible thankfulness. But I feel no chains, and am in no prison. I received my freedom from Heaven, and with it came the command to defend my title to it. I have long since resolved to do nothing and suffer nothing that can, in any way, imply that I am indebted to any power but the Almighty for my manhood and personality.

Now, you are assembled here, the strength of this city is here to express their sense of this fugitive act, and to proclaim to the despots at Washington whether it shall be enforced here—whether you will permit the government to return me and other fugitives who have sought asylum among you, to the Hell of slavery. The question is with you. If you will give us up, say so, and we will shake the dust from our feet and leave you. But we believe better things. We know you are taken by surprise. The immensity of this meeting testifies to the general consternation that has brought it together, necessarily, precipitately, to decide the most stirring question that can be presented, to wit, whether, the government having transgressed Constitutional and natural limits, you will bravely resist its aggressions, and tell its soulless agents that no slaveholder shall make your city and county a hunting field for slaves.

Whatever may be your decision, my ground is taken. I have declared it everywhere. It is known over the state and out of the state—over the line in the North, and over the line in the South. I don't respect this law—I don't fear it—I won't obey it! It outlaws me, and I outlaw it, and the men who attempt to enforce it on me. I place the governmental officials on the ground that they place me. I will not live a slave, and if force is employed to reenslave me, I shall make preparations to meet the crisis as becomes a man. If you will stand by me—and I believe you will do it, for your freedom and honor are involved as well as mine—it requires no microscope to see that—I say if you will stand with us in resistance to this measure, you will be the saviors of your country. Your decision tonight in favor of resistance will give vent to the spirit of liberty, and it will break the bands of party, and shout for joy all over the North. Your example only is needed to be the type of popular action in Auburn, and Rochester, and Utica, and Buffalo, and all the West, and eventually in the Atlantic cities. Heaven knows that this act of noble daring will break out somewhere—and may God grant that Syracuse be the honored spot, whence it shall send an earthquake voice through the land!

Sojourner Truth

(1797–1883)

AIN'T I A WOMAN?
May 29, 1851

Sojourner Truth, born Isabella Baumfree, was a slave in Ulster County, New York, until gaining her freedom in 1827—mere months before New York State abolished slavery forever. In 1843 she took the name Sojourner Truth and began her noted career as an abolitionist and feminist. The following speech was given by Truth at a women's rights convention in Akron, Ohio. It was offered largely in response to a clergyman who had previously argued that women were too weak and helpless to be given the right to vote.

WELL, CHILDREN, where there is so much racket there must be something out of kilter. I think that 'twixt the Negroes of the South and the women at the North, all talking about rights, the white men will be in a fix pretty soon. But what's all this here talking about?

That man over there says that women need to be helped into carriages, and lifted over ditches, and to have the best place everywhere. Nobody ever helps me into carriages, or over mud-puddles, or gives me any best place! And ain't I a woman? Look at me! Look at my arm! I have ploughed and planted, and gathered into barns, and no man could head me! And ain't I a woman? I could work as much and eat as much as a man—when I could get it—and bear the lash as well! And ain't I a woman? I have borne thirteen children, and seen most all sold off to slavery, and when I cried out with my mother's grief, none but Jesus heard me! And ain't I a woman?

Then they talk about this thing in the head; what's this they call it? [member of audience whispers, "intellect"] That's it, honey. What's that got to do with women's rights or Negroes' rights? If my cup won't hold but a pint, and yours holds a quart, wouldn't you be mean not to let me have my little half measure full?

Then that little man in black there, he says women can't have as much rights as men, 'cause Christ wasn't a woman! Where did your Christ come from? Where did your Christ come from? From God and a woman! Man had nothing to do with Him.

If the first woman God ever made was strong enough to turn the world upside down all alone, these women together ought to be able to turn it back, and get it right side up again! And now they is asking to do it, the men better let them.

Obliged to you for hearing me, and now old Sojourner ain't got nothing more to say.

Frederick Douglass

(1818–1895)

WHAT, TO THE SLAVE,
IS THE FOURTH OF JULY?

July 5, 1852

*Frederick Douglass was born to a slave mother and a white father; he imme-
diately was sent to live with his grandmother on a plantation in Maryland.
From the ages of eight to sixteen, he was sent to be a house servant in
Baltimore, where he was taught to read by his master's wife. Douglass escaped
slavery in 1838 and was given the position of agent for the Massachusetts
Anti-Slavery Society in 1841—thus beginning his long career as an abolitionist. Douglass delivered this speech in Rochester, New York, at the city's
annual Fourth of July celebration.*

MR. PRESIDENT, friends and fellow citizens: He who could address this
audience without a quailing sensation, has stronger nerves than I have. I
do not remember ever to have appeared as a speaker before any assembly more shrinkingly, nor with greater distrust of my ability, than I do this
day. A feeling has crept over me quite unfavorable to the exercise of my
limited powers of speech. The task before me is one which requires
much previous thought and study for its proper performance. I know
that apologies of this sort are generally considered flat and unmeaning. I
trust, however, that mine will not be so considered. Should I seem at
ease, my appearance would much misrepresent me. The little experience
I have had in addressing public meetings, in country school houses, avails
me nothing on the present occasion.

The papers and placards say that I am to deliver a Fourth [of] July ora-
tion. This certainly sounds large, and out of the common way, for me. It
is true that I have often had the privilege to speak in this beautiful
Hall, and to address many who now honor me with their presence. But

neither their familiar faces, nor the perfect gauge I think I have of Corinthian Hall seems to free me from embarrassment.

The fact is, ladies and gentlemen, the distance between this platform and the slave plantation, from which I escaped, is considerable—and the difficulties to be overcome in getting from the latter to the former are by no means slight. That I am here today is, to me, a matter of astonishment as well as of gratitude. You will not, therefore, be surprised, if in what I have to say I evince no elaborate preparation, nor grace my speech with any high-sounding exordium. With little experience and with less learning, I have been able to throw my thoughts hastily and imperfectly together; and trusting to your patient and generous indulgence, I will proceed to lay them before you.

This, for the purpose of this celebration, is the Fourth of July. It is the birthday of your National Independence, and of your political freedom. This, to you, is what the Passover was to the emancipated people of God. It carries your minds back to the day, and to the act of your great deliverance; and to the signs and to the wonders associated with that act and that day. This celebration also marks the beginning of another year of your national life; and reminds you that the Republic of America is now seventy-six years old. I am glad, fellow citizens, that your nation is so young. Seventy-six years, though a good old age for a man, is but a mere speck in the life of a nation. Three score years and ten is the allotted time for individual men; but nations number their years by thousands. According to this fact, you are, even now, only in the beginning of your national career, still lingering in the period of childhood. I repeat, I am glad this is so. There is hope in the thought, and hope is much needed, under the dark clouds which lower above the horizon. The eye of the reformer is met with angry flashes, portending disastrous times; but his heart may well beat lighter at the thought that America is young, and that she is still in the impressible stage of her existence. May he not hope that high lessons of wisdom, of justice and of truth, will yet give direction to her destiny? Were the nation older, the patriot's heart might be sadder and the reformer's brow heavier. Its future might be shrouded in gloom and the hope of its prophets go out in sorrow. There is consolation in the thought that America is young. Great streams are not easily turned from channels worn deep in the course of ages. They may sometimes rise in quiet and stately majesty, and inundate the land, refreshing and fertilizing the earth with their mysterious properties. They may also rise in wrath and fury, and bear away on their angry waves the accumulated wealth of years of toil and hardship. They, however, gradually flow back to the same old channel and flow on as serenely as ever. But, while the river may not be turned aside, it may dry up and leave nothing behind but the withered branch and the unsightly rock, to howl in the abyss-sweeping wind, the sad tale of departed glory. As with rivers, so with nations.

Fellow citizens, I shall not presume to dwell at length on the associations that cluster about this day. The simple story of it is, that seventy-six years ago the people of this country were British subjects. The style and title of your "sovereign people" (in which you now glory) was not then born. You were under the British Crown. Your fathers esteemed the English government as the home government, and England as the fatherland. This home government, you know, although a considerable distance from your home, did, in the exercise of its parental prerogatives, impose upon its colonial children such restraints, burdens and limitations, as, in its mature judgment, it deemed wise, right and proper.

But your fathers, who had not adopted the fashionable idea of this day, of the infallibility of government and the absolute character of its acts, presumed to differ from the home government in respect to the wisdom and the justice of some of those burdens and restraints. They went so far in their excitement as to pronounce the measures of government unjust, unreasonable and oppressive, and altogether such as ought not to be quietly submitted to. I scarcely need say, fellow citizens, that my opinion of those measures fully accords with that of your fathers. Such a declaration of agreement on my part would not be worth much to anybody. It would certainly prove nothing as to what part I might have taken had I lived during the great controversy of 1776. To say now that America was right and England wrong is exceedingly easy. Everybody can say it; the dastard, not less than the noble brave, can flippantly discant on the tyranny of England toward the American colonies. It is fashionable to do so; but there was a time when to pronounce against England and in favor of the cause of the colonies tried men's souls. They who did so were accounted in their day plotters of mischief, agitators and rebels, dangerous men. To side with the right against the wrong, with the weak against the strong, and with the oppressed against the oppressor— here lies the merit, and the one which, of all others, seems unfashionable in our day. The cause of liberty may be stabbed by the men who glory in the deeds of your fathers. But, to proceed.

Feeling themselves harshly and unjustly treated by the home government, your fathers, like men of honesty and men of spirit, earnestly sought redress. They petitioned and remonstrated; they did so in a decorous, respectful and loyal manner. Their conduct was wholly unexceptionable. This, however, did not answer the purpose. They saw themselves treated with sovereign indifference, coldness and scorn. Yet they persevered. They were not the men to look back.

As the sheet anchor takes a firmer hold when the ship is tossed by the storm, so did the cause of your fathers grow stronger as it breasted the chilling blasts of kingly displeasure. The greatest and best of British statesmen admitted its justice, and the loftiest eloquence of the British Senate came to its support. But, with that blindness which seems to be the unvarying characteristic of tyrants, since Pharaoh and his hosts were drowned in the Red Sea, the British government persisted in the exactions complained of.

The madness of this course, we believe, is admitted now, even by England; but we fear the lesson is wholly lost on our present rulers.

Oppression makes a wise man mad. Your fathers were wise men, and if they did not go mad, they became restive under this treatment. They felt themselves the victims of grievous wrongs, wholly incurable in their colonial capacity. With brave men there is always a remedy for oppression. Just here, the idea of a total separation of the colonies from the Crown was born! It was a startling idea, much more so than we at this distance of time regard it. The timid and the prudent (as has been intimated) of that day were, of course, shocked and alarmed by it.

Such people lived then, had lived before and will, probably, ever have a place on this planet; and their course, in respect to any great change (no matter how great the good to be attained, or the wrong to be redressed by it), may be calculated with as much precision as can be the course of the stars. They hate all changes, but silver, gold and copper change! Of this sort of change they are always strongly in favor.

These people were called tories in the days of your fathers; and the appellation probably conveyed the same idea that is meant by a more modern, though a somewhat less euphonious term, which we often find in our papers, applied to some of our old politicians.

Their opposition to the then dangerous thought was earnest and powerful; but, amid all their terror and affrighted vociferations against it, the alarming and revolutionary idea moved on, and the country with it.

On the second of July, 1776, the old Continental Congress, to the dismay of the lovers of ease, and the worshipers of property, clothed that dreadful idea with all the authority of national sanction. They did so in the form of a resolution; and as we seldom hit upon resolutions drawn up in our day whose transparency is at all equal to this, it may refresh your minds and help my story if I read it.

[We] solemnly publish and declare, That these United Colonies are, and of Right, ought to be Free and Independent States; that they are Absolved from all Allegiance to the British Crown, and that all political connection between them and the State of Great Britain is and ought to be [totally] dissolved.

Citizens, your fathers made good that resolution. They succeeded; and today you reap the fruits of their success. The freedom gained is yours;

and you, therefore, may properly celebrate this anniversary. The Fourth of July is the first great fact in your nation's history—the very ringbolt in the chain of your yet undeveloped destiny.

Pride and patriotism, not less than gratitude, prompt you to celebrate and to hold it in perpetual remembrance. I have said that the Declaration of Independence is the ringbolt to the chain of your nation's destiny; so, indeed, I regard it. The principles contained in that instrument are saving principles. Stand by those principles, be true to them on all occasions, in all places, against all foes, and at whatever cost.

From the round top of your ship of state, dark and threatening clouds may be seen. Heavy billows, like mountains in the distance, disclose to the leeward huge forms of flinty rocks! That bolt drawn, that chain broken, and all is lost. Cling to this day—cling to it, and to its principles, with the grasp of a storm-tossed mariner to a spar at midnight.

The coming into being of a nation, in any circumstances, is an interesting event. But, besides general considerations, there were peculiar circumstances which make the advent of this republic an event of special attractiveness.

The whole scene, as I look back to it, was simple, dignified and sublime. The population of the country, at the time, stood at the insignificant number of three millions. The country was poor in the munitions of war. The population was weak and scattered, and the country a wilderness unsubdued. There were then no means of concert and combination, such as exist now. Neither steam nor lightning had then been reduced to order and discipline. From the Potomac to the Delaware was a journey of many days. Under these and innumerable other disadvantages, your fathers declared for liberty and independence and triumphed.

Fellow citizens, I am not wanting in respect for the fathers of this republic. The signers of the Declaration of Independence were brave men. They were great men, too—great enough to give frame to a great age. It does not often happen to a nation to raise, at one time, such a number of truly great men. The point from which I am compelled to view them is not, certainly, the most favorable; and yet I cannot contemplate their great deeds with less than admiration. They were statesmen, patriots and heroes, and for the good they did, and the principles they contended for, I will unite with you to honor their memory.

They loved their country better than their own private interests; and, though this is not the highest form of human excellence, all will concede that it is a rare virtue, and that when it is exhibited, it ought to command respect. He who will intelligently lay down his life for his country is a man whom it is not in human nature to despise. Your fathers staked their lives, their fortunes and their sacred honor on the cause of their country. In their admiration of liberty, they lost sight of all other interests.

They were peace men; but they preferred revolution to peaceful sub-mission to bondage. They were quiet men; but they did not shrink from agitating against oppression. They showed forbearance, but that they knew its limits. They believed in order, but not in the order of tyranny. With them, nothing was "settled" that was not right. With them, justice, liberty and humanity were "final," not slavery and oppression. You may well cherish the memory of such men. They were great in their day and generation. Their solid manhood stands out the more as we contrast it with these degenerate times.

How circumspect, exact and proportionate were all their movements! How unlike the politicians of an hour! Their statesmanship looked beyond the passing moment, and stretched away in strength into the distant future. They seized upon eternal principles and set a glorious example in their defense. Mark them!

Fully appreciating the hardship to be encountered, firmly believing in the right of their cause, honorably inviting the scrutiny of an on-looking world, reverently appealing to heaven to attest their sincerity, soundly comprehending the solemn responsibility they were about to assume, wisely measuring the terrible odds against them, your fathers, the fathers of this republic, did most deliberately, under the inspiration of a glorious patriotism and with a sublime faith in the great principles of justice and freedom, lay deep the cornerstone of the national superstructure, which has risen and still rises in grandeur around you.

Of this fundamental work, this day is the anniversary. Our eyes are met with demonstrations of joyous enthusiasm. Banners and pennants wave exultingly on the breeze. The din of business too is hushed. Even Mammon seems to have quitted his grasp on this day. The ear-piercing fife and the stirring drum unite their accents with the ascending peal of a thousand church bells. Prayers are made, hymns are sung and sermons are preached in honor of this day; while the quick martial tramp of a great and multitudinous nation, echoes back by all the hills, valleys and mountains of a vast continent, bespeak the occasion one of thrilling and universal interest—a nation's jubilee.

Friends and citizens, I need not enter further into the causes which led to this anniversary. Many of you understand them better than I do. You could instruct me in regard to them. That is a branch of knowledge in which you feel, perhaps, a much deeper interest than your speaker. The causes which led to the separation of the colonies from the British Crown have never lacked for a tongue. They have all been taught in your com-mon schools, narrated at your firesides, unfolded from your pulpits, and thundered from your legislative halls, and are as familiar to you as house-hold words. They form the staple of your national poetry and eloquence.

I remember also that as a people Americans are remarkably familiar with all facts which make in their own favor. This is esteemed by some as a national trait—perhaps a national weakness. It is a fact that whatever makes for the wealth or for the reputation of Americans and can be had cheap will be found by Americans. I shall not be charged with slandering Americans if I say I think the American side of any question may be safely left in American hands.

I leave, therefore, the great deeds of your fathers to other gentlemen whose claim to have been regularly descended will be less likely to be disputed than mine!

My business, if I have any here today, is with the present. The accepted time with God and His cause is the ever-living now.

> *Trust no future, however pleasant,*
> *Let the dead past bury its dead;*
> *Act, act in the living present,*
> *Heart within, and God overhead.*

We have to do with the past only as we can make it useful to the present and to the future. To all inspiring motives, to noble deeds which can be gained from the past, we are welcome. But now is the time, the important time. Your fathers have lived, died, and have done their work, and have done much of it well. You live and must die, and you must do your work. You have no right to enjoy a child's share in the labor of your fathers, unless your children are to be blest by your labors. You have no right to wear out and waste the hard-earned fame of your fathers to cover your indolence. Sydney Smith tells us that men seldom eulogize the wisdom and virtues of their fathers, but to excuse some folly or wickedness of their own. This truth is not a doubtful one. There are illustrations of it near and remote, ancient and modern. It was fashionable, hundreds of years ago, for the children of Jacob to boast, we have "Abraham to our father," when they had long lost Abraham's faith and spirit. That people contented themselves under the shadow of Abraham's great name, while they repudiated the deeds which made his name great. Need I remind you that a similar thing is being done all over this country today? Need I tell you that the Jews are not the only people who built the tombs of the prophets, and garnished the sepulchers of the righteous? Washington could not die till he had broken the chains of his slaves. Yet his monument is built up by the price of human blood, and the traders in the bodies and souls of men shout—"We have Washington to *our father*."—Alas! that it should be so; yet so it is.

> *The evil that men do, lives after them,*
> *The good is oft interred with their bones.*

Fellow citizens, pardon me, allow me to ask, why am I called upon to speak here today? What have I, or those I represent, to do with your national independence? Are the great principles of political freedom and of natural justice, embodied in that Declaration of Independence, extended to us? and am I, therefore, called upon to bring our humble offering to the national altar and to confess the benefits and express devout gratitude for the blessings resulting from your independence to us?

Would to God, both for your sakes and ours, that an affirmative answer could be truthfully returned to these questions! Then would my task be light and my burden easy and delightful. For *who* is there so cold that a nation's sympathy could not warm him? Who so obdurate and dead to the claims of gratitude that would not thankfully acknowledge such priceless benefits? Who so stolid and selfish that would not give his voice to swell the hallelujahs of a nation's jubilee, when the chains of servitude had been torn from his limbs? I am not that man. In a case like that, the dumb might eloquently speak, and the "lame man leap as an hart."

But such is not the state of the case. I say it with a sad sense of the disparity between us. I am not included within the pale of this glorious anniversary! Your high independence only reveals the immeasurable distance between us. The blessings in which you, this day, rejoice, are not enjoyed in common. The rich inheritance of justice, liberty, prosperity and independence, bequeathed by your fathers, is shared by you, not by me. The sunlight that brought light and healing to you, has brought stripes and death to me. This Fourth of July is *yours,* not *mine. You* may rejoice, *I* must mourn. To drag a man in fetters into the grand illuminated temple of liberty and call upon him to join you in joyous anthems were inhuman mockery and sacrilegious irony. Do you mean, citizens, to mock me, by asking me to speak today? If so, there is a parallel to your conduct. And let me warn you that it is dangerous to copy the example of a nation whose crimes, towering up to heaven, were thrown down by the breath of the Almighty, burying that nation in irrecoverable ruin! I can today take up the plaintive lament of a peeled and woe-smitten people!

"By the rivers of Babylon, there we sat down. Yea! we wept when we remembered Zion. We hanged our harps upon the willows in the midst thereof. For there they that carried us away captive required of us a song; and they who wasted us required of us mirth, saying, Sing us one of the songs of Zion. How shall we sing the Lord's song in a strange land? If I forget thee, O Jerusalem, let my right hand forget her cunning. If I do not remember thee, let my tongue cleave to the roof of my mouth."

Fellow citizens; above your national, tumultuous joy I hear the mournful wail of millions! whose chains, heavy and grievous yesterday, are today rendered more intolerable by the jubilee shouts that reach them. If I do forget, if I do not faithfully remember those bleeding children of sorrow this day, "may my right hand forget her cunning, and may my tongue cleave to the roof of my mouth!" To forget them, to pass lightly over their wrongs and to chime in with the popular theme would be treason most scandalous and shocking and would make me a reproach before God and the world. My subject, then, fellow citizens, is American slavery. I shall see this day and its popular characteristics from the slave's point of view. Standing there identified with the American bondman, making his wrongs mine, I do not hesitate to declare, with all my soul, that the character and conduct of this nation never looked blacker to me than on this Fourth of July. Whether we turn to the declarations of the past or to the professions of the present, the conduct of the nation seems equally hideous and revolting. America is false to the past, false to the present, and solemnly binds herself to be false to the future. Standing with God and the crushed and bleeding slave on this occasion, I will, in the name of humanity which is outraged, in the name of liberty which is fettered, in the name of the Constitution and the Bible which are disregarded and trampled upon, dare to call in question and to denounce, with all the emphasis I can command, everything that serves to perpetuate slavery—the great sin and shame of America! "I will not equivocate; I will not excuse"; I will use the severest language I can command; and yet not one word shall escape me that any man, whose judgment is not blinded by prejudice, or who is not at heart a slaveholder, shall not confess to be right and just.

But I fancy I hear some one of my audience say, "It is just in this circumstance that you and your brother abolitionists fail to make a favorable impression on the public mind. Would you argue more and denounce less, would you persuade more and rebuke less, your cause would be much more likely to succeed." But, I submit, where all is plain there is nothing to be argued. What point in the antislavery creed would you have me argue? On what branch of the subject do the people of this country need light? Must I undertake to prove that the slave is a man? That point is conceded already. Nobody doubts it. The slaveholders themselves acknowledge it in the enactment of laws for their government. They acknowledge it when they punish disobedience on the part of the slave. There are seventy-two crimes in the state of Virginia which, if committed by a black man (no matter how ignorant he be), subject him to the punishment of death; while only two of the same crimes will subject a white man to the like punishment. What is this but the acknowledgement that the slave is a moral, intellectual and responsible being? The manhood of the slave is conceded. It is admitted in the fact that Southern statute books are covered with enactments forbidding, under severe fines and penalties, the teaching of the slave to read or to write. When you can point to any such laws in reference to the beasts of the field, then I may consent to argue the manhood of the slave. When the dogs in your streets, when the fowls of the air, when the cattle on your hills, when the fish of the sea and the reptiles that crawl shall be unable to distinguish the slave from a brute, *then* will I argue with you that the slave is a man!

For the present, it is enough to affirm the equal manhood of the Negro race. Is it not astonishing that, while we are plowing, planting and reaping, using all kinds of mechanical tools, erecting houses, constructing bridges, building ships, working in metals of brass, iron, copper, silver and gold; that, while we are reading, writing and ciphering, acting as clerks, merchants and secretaries, having among us lawyers, doctors, ministers, poets, authors, editors, orators and teachers; that, while we are engaged in all manner of enterprises common to other men, digging gold in California, capturing the whale in the Pacific, feeding sheep and cattle on the hillside, living, moving, acting, thinking, planning, living in families as husbands, wives and children, and, above all, confessing and worshiping the Christian's God and looking hopefully for life and immortality beyond the grave, we are called upon to prove that we are men!

Would you have me argue that man is entitled to liberty? that he is the rightful owner of his own body? You have already declared it. Must I argue the wrongfulness of slavery? Is that a question for republicans? Is it to be settled by the rules of logic and argumentation, as a matter beset with great difficulty, involving a doubtful application of the principle of justice, hard to be understood? How should I look today, in the presence of Americans, dividing and subdividing a discourse, to show that men have a natural right to freedom, speaking of it relatively and positively, negatively and affirmatively? To do so would be to make myself ridiculous and to offer an insult to your understanding. There is not a man beneath the canopy of heaven that does not know that slavery is wrong *for him*.

What, am I to argue that it is wrong to make men brutes, to rob them of their liberty, to work them without wages, to keep them ignorant of their relations to their fellow men, to beat them with sticks, to flay their flesh with the lash, to load their limbs with irons, to hunt them with dogs, to sell them at auction, to sunder their families, to knock out their teeth, to burn their flesh, to starve them into obedience and submission to their masters? Must I argue that a system thus marked with blood and stained with pollution is *wrong?* No! I will not. I have better employments for my time and strength than such arguments would imply.

What, then, remains to be argued? Is it that slavery is not divine; that God did not establish it; that our doctors of divinity are mistaken? There is blasphemy in the thought. That which is inhuman, cannot be divine! *Who* can reason on such a proposition? They that can, may; I cannot. The time for such argument is passed.

At a time like this, scorching irony, not convincing argument, is needed. O! had I the ability, and could I reach the nation's ear, I would, today, pour out a fiery stream of biting ridicule, blasting reproach, withering sarcasm and stern rebuke. For it is not light that is needed, but fire; it is not the gentle shower, but thunder. We need the storm, the whirlwind, and the earthquake. The feeling of the nation must be quickened; the conscience of the nation must be roused; the propriety of the nation must be startled; the hypocrisy of the nation must be exposed; and its crimes against God and man must be proclaimed and denounced.

What, to the American slave, is your Fourth of July? I answer: a day that reveals to him, more than all other days in the year, the gross injustice and cruelty to which he is the constant victim. To him, your celebration is a sham; your boasted liberty an unholy license; your national greatness swelling vanity; your sounds of rejoicing are empty and heartless; your denunciations of tyrants brass-fronted impudence; your shouts of liberty and equality hollow mockery; your prayers and hymns, your sermons and thanksgivings, with all your religious parade and solemnity, are to Him mere bombast, fraud, deception, impiety and hypocrisy—a thin veil to cover up crimes which would disgrace a nation of savages. There is not a nation on the earth guilty of practices more shocking and bloody than are the people of the United States at this very hour.

Go where you may, search where you will, roam through all the monarchies and despotisms of the Old World, travel through South America, search out every abuse, and when you have found the last, lay your facts by the side of the everyday practices of this nation, and you will say with me, that, for revolting barbarity and shameless hypocrisy, America reigns without a rival.

Take the American slave trade, which, we are told by the papers, is especially prosperous just now. Ex-Senator Benton tells us that the price of men was never higher than now. He mentions the fact to show that slavery is in no danger. This trade is one of the peculiarities of American institutions. It is carried on in all the large towns and cities in one half of this confederacy; and millions are pocketed every year by dealers in this horrid traffic. In several states, this trade is a chief source of wealth. It is called (in contradistinction to the foreign slave trade) *"the internal slave trade."* It is probably called so, too, in order to divert from it the horror with which the foreign slave trade is contemplated. That trade has long since been denounced by this government as piracy. It has been denounced with burning words from the high places of the nation as an execrable traffic. To arrest it, to put an end to it, this nation keeps a squadron, at immense cost, on the coast of Africa. Everywhere in this country it is safe to speak of this foreign slave trade as a most inhuman traffic, opposed alike to the laws of God and of man. The duty to extirpate and destroy it is admitted even by our doctors of divinity. In order to put an end to it, some of these last have consented that their colored brethren (nominally free) should leave this country, and establish themselves on the western coast of Africa! It is, however, a notable fact that, while so much execration is poured out by Americans upon all those engaged in the foreign slave trade, the men engaged in the slave trade between the states pass without condemnation, and their business is deemed honorable.

Behold the practical operation of this internal slave trade, the American slave trade, sustained by American politics and American religion. Here you will see men and women reared like swine for the market. You know what is a swine-drover? I will show you a man-drover. They inhabit all our Southern states. They perambulate the country and crowd the highways of the nation with droves of human stock. You will see one of these human flesh jobbers, armed with pistol, whip and bowie knife, driving a company of a hundred men, women and children, from the Potomac to the slave market at New Orleans. These wretched people are to be sold singly or in lots, to suit purchasers. They are food for the cotton field and the deadly sugar mill. Mark the sad procession, as it moves wearily along, and the inhuman wretch who drives them. Hear his savage yells and his blood-curdling oaths, as he hurries on his affrighted captives! There, see the old man with locks thinned and gray. Cast one glance, if you please, upon that young mother, whose shoulders are bare to the scorching sun, her briny tears falling on the brow of the babe in her arms. See, too, that girl of thirteen, weeping—*yes,* weeping—as she thinks of the mother from whom she has been torn! The drove moves tardily. Heat and sorrow have nearly consumed their strength; suddenly you hear a quick snap, like the discharge of a rifle; the fetters clank, and the chain rattles simultaneously; your ears are saluted with a scream, that seems to have torn its way to the center of your soul! The crack you heard was the sound of the slave whip; the scream you heard was from the woman you saw with the babe. Her speed had faltered under the weight of her child and her chains! That gash on her shoulder tells her to move on. Follow this drove to New Orleans. Attend the auction; see men examined like horses; see the forms of women rudely and brutally exposed to the shocking gaze of American slave buyers. See this drove sold and separated forever; and never forget the deep, sad sobs that arose from that scattered multitude. Tell me, citizens, where, under the sun, you can witness a spectacle more fiendish and shocking. Yet this is but a glance at the American slave trade, as it exists, at this moment, in the ruling part of the United States.

I was born amid such sights and scenes. To me the American slave trade is a terrible reality. When a child, my soul was often pierced with a sense of its horrors. I lived on Philpot Street, Fell's Point, Baltimore, and have watched from the wharves the slave ships in the Basin, anchored from the shore, with their cargoes of human flesh, waiting for favorable winds to waft them down the Chesapeake. There was at that time a grand slave mart kept at the head of Pratt Street by Austin Woldfolk. His agents were sent into every town and county in Maryland, announcing their arrival, through the papers, and on flaming *handbills* headed "Cash for Negroes." These men were generally well-dressed men, and very captivating in their manners; ever ready to drink, to treat and to gamble. The fate of many a slave has depended upon the turn of a single card; and many a child has been snatched from the arms of its mother by bargains arranged in a state of brutal drunkenness.

The flesh mongers gather up their victims by dozens, and drive them, chained, to the general depot at Baltimore. When a sufficient number have been collected here, a ship is chartered for the purpose of conveying the forlorn crew to Mobile, or to New Orleans. From the slave prison to the ship, they are usually driven in the darkness of night; for since the antislavery agitation a certain caution is observed.

In the deep, still darkness of midnight I have been often aroused by the dead, heavy footsteps and the piteous cries of the chained gangs that passed our door. The anguish of my boyish heart was intense; and I was often consoled, when speaking to my mistress in the morning, to hear her say that the custom was very wicked; that she hated to hear the rattle of the chains and the heart-rending cries. I was glad to find one who sympathized with me in my horror.

Fellow citizens, this murderous traffic is today in active operation in this boasted republic. In the solitude of my spirit I see clouds of dust raised on the highways of the South; I see the bleeding footsteps; I hear the doleful wail of fettered humanity on the way to the slave markets, where the victims are to be sold like *horses, sheep* and *swine,* knocked off to the highest bidder. There I see the tenderest ties ruthlessly broken, to gratify the lust, caprice and rapacity of the buyers and sellers of men. My soul sickens at the sight.

> Is this the land your Fathers loved,
>   The freedom which they toiled to win?
> Is this the earth whereon they moved?
>   Are these the graves they slumber in?

But a still more inhuman, disgraceful and scandalous state of things remains to be presented. By an act of the American congress, not yet two years old, slavery has been nationalized in its most horrible and revolting form. By that act, Mason and Dixon's line has been obliterated; New

York has become as Virginia; and the power to hold, hunt and sell men, women and children as slaves remains no longer a mere state institution, but is now an institution of the whole United States. The power is coextensive with the star-spangled banner and American Christianity. Where these go, may also go the merciless slave hunter. Where these are, man is not sacred. He is a bird for the sportsman's gun. By that most foul and fiendish of all human decrees, the liberty and person of every man are put in peril. Your broad republican domain is hunting ground for *men*. Not for thieves and robbers, enemies of society, merely, but for men guilty of no crime. Your lawmakers have commanded all good citizens to engage in this hellish sport. Your President, your Secretary of State, your *lords, nobles* and ecclesiastics enforce, as a duty you owe to your free and glorious country, and to your God, that you do this accursed thing. Not fewer than forty Americans have, within the past two years, been hunted down and, without a moment's warning, hurried away in chains and consigned to slavery and excruciating torture. Some of these have had wives and children, dependent on them for bread; but of this, no account was made. The right of the hunter to his prey stands superior to the right of marriage and to *all* rights in this republic, the rights of God included! For black men there are neither law nor justice, humanity nor religion. The Fugitive Slave *Law* makes mercy to them a crime; and bribes the judge who tries them. An American judge gets ten dollars for every victim he consigns to slavery, and five, when he fails to do so. The oath of any two villains is sufficient, under this hell-black enactment, to send the most pious and exemplary black man into the remorseless jaws of slavery! His own testimony is nothing. He can bring no witnesses for himself. The minister of American justice is bound by the law to hear but *one* side; and *that* side is the side of the oppressor. Let this damning fact be perpetually told. Let it be thundered around the world that in tyrant-killing, king-hating, people-loving, democratic, Christian America the seats of justice are filled with judges who hold their offices under an open and palpable *bribe,* and are bound, in deciding in the case of a man's liberty, *to hear only his accusers!*

In glaring violation of justice, in shameless disregard of the forms of administering law, in cunning arrangement to entrap the defenseless, and in diabolical intent, this Fugitive Slave Law stands alone in the annals of tyrannical legislation. I doubt if there be another nation on the globe having the brass and the baseness to put such a law on the statute book. If any man in this assembly thinks differently from me in this matter and feels able to disprove my statements, I will gladly confront him at any suitable time and place he may select.

I take this law to be one of the grossest infringements of Christian liberty, and if the churches and ministers of our country were not stupidly blind or most wickedly indifferent, they too would so regard it.

At the very moment that they are thanking God for the enjoyment of civil and religious liberty, and for the right to worship God according to the dictates of their own consciences, they are utterly silent in respect to a law which robs religion of its chief significance and makes it utterly worthless to a world lying in wickedness. Did this law concern the *"mint, anise and cummin,"* abridge the right to sing psalms, to partake of the sacrament or to engage in any of the ceremonies of religion, it would be smitten by the thunder of a thousand pulpits. A general shout would go up from the church demanding *repeal, repeal, instant repeal!* And it would go hard with that politician who presumed to solicit the votes of the people without inscribing this motto on his banner. Further, if this demand were not complied with, another Scotland would be added to the history of religious liberty, and the stern old covenanters would be thrown into the shade. A John Knox would be seen at every church door and heard from every pulpit, and Fillmore would have no more quarter than was shown by Knox to the beautiful, but treacherous, Queen Mary of Scotland. The fact that the church of our country (with fractional exceptions) does not esteem "the Fugitive Slave Law" as a declaration of war against religious liberty, implies that that church regards religion simply as a form of worship, an empty ceremony, and *not* a vital principle, requiring active benevolence, justice, love and good will towards man. It esteems sacrifice above mercy, psalm singing above right doing, solemn meetings above practical righteousness. A worship that can be conducted by persons who refuse to give shelter to the houseless, to give bread to the hungry, clothing to the naked, and who enjoin obedience to a law forbidding these acts of mercy is a curse, not a blessing to mankind. The Bible addresses all such persons as "scribes, pharisees, hypocrites, who pay tithe of *mint, anise* and *cummin,* and have omitted the weightier matters of the law, judgment, mercy and faith."

But the church of this country is not only indifferent to the wrongs of the slave, it actually takes sides with the oppressors. It has made itself the bulwark of American slavery and the shield of American slave hunters. Many of its most eloquent divines, who stand as the very lights of the church, have shamelessly given the sanction of religion and the Bible to the whole slave system. They have taught that man may, properly, be a slave; that the relation of master and slave is ordained of God; that to send back an escaped bondman to his master is clearly the duty of all the followers of the Lord Jesus Christ; and this horrible blasphemy is palmed off upon the world for Christianity.

For my part, I would say, Welcome infidelity! welcome atheism! welcome anything—in preference to the gospel, *as preached by those divines.* They convert the very name of religion into an engine of tyranny and barbarous cruelty, and serve to confirm more infidels, in this age, than all the infidel writings of Thomas Paine, Voltaire and Bolingbroke put together have done! These ministers make religion a cold and flinty-hearted thing, having neither principles of right action nor bowels of compassion. They strip the love of God of its beauty and leave the throne of religion a huge, horrible, repulsive form. It is a religion for oppressors, tyrants, man stealers, and *thugs.* It is not that *"pure and undefiled religion"* which is from above, and which is *"first pure, then peaceable, easy to be entreated,* full of mercy and good fruits, *without partiality and without hypocrisy,"* but a religion which favors the rich against the poor; which exalts the proud above the humble; which divides mankind into two classes, tyrants and slaves; which says to the man in chains, *stay there,* and to the oppressor, *oppress on;* it is a religion which may be professed and enjoyed by all the robbers and enslavers of mankind; it makes God a respecter of persons, denies his fatherhood of the race, and tramples in the dust the great truth of the brotherhood of man. All this we affirm to be true of the popular church, and the popular worship of our land and nation—a religion, a church, and a worship which, on the authority of inspired wisdom, we pronounce to be an abomination in the sight of God. In the language of Isaiah, the American church might be well addressed, "Bring no more vain ablations; incense is an abomination unto me: the new moons and Sabbaths, the calling of assemblies, I cannot away with; it is iniquity, even the solemn meeting. Your new moons, and your appointed feasts my soul hateth. They are a trouble to me; I am weary to bear them; and when ye spread forth your hands I will hide mine eyes from you. Yea! when ye make many prayers, I will not hear. *Your hands are full of blood;* cease to do evil, learn to do well; seek judgment; relieve the oppressed; judge for the fatherless; plead for the widow."

The American church is guilty, when viewed in connection with what it is doing to uphold slavery; but it is superlatively guilty when viewed in connection with its ability to abolish slavery.

The sin of which it is guilty is one of omission as well as of commission. Albert Barnes but uttered what the common sense of every man at all observant of the actual state of the case will receive as truth, when he declared that "there is no power out of the church that could sustain slavery an hour, if it were not sustained in it."

Let the religious press, the pulpit, the Sunday school, the conference meeting, the great ecclesiastical, missionary, Bible and tract associations of the land array their immense powers against slavery and slave holding; and the whole system of crime and blood would be scattered to the winds, and that they do not do this involves them in the most awful responsibility of which the mind can conceive.

In prosecuting the antislavery enterprise, we have been asked to spare the church, to spare the ministry; but *how,* we ask, could such a thing be done? We are met on the threshold of our efforts for the redemption of the slave, by the church and ministry of the country, in battle arrayed against us; and we are compelled to fight or flee. From *what* quarter, I beg to know, has proceeded a fire so deadly upon our ranks, during the last two years, as from the Northern pulpit? As the champions of oppressors, the chosen men of American theology have appeared—men honored for their so-called piety, and their real learning. The Lords of Buffalo, the Springs of New York, the Lathrops of Auburn, the Coxes and Spencers of Brooklyn, the Gannets and Sharps of Boston, the Deweys of Washington, and other great religious lights of the land have, in utter denial of the authority of *Him* by whom they professed to be called to the ministry, deliberately taught us, against the example of the Hebrews and against the remonstrance of the Apostles, *that we ought to obey man's law before the law of God.*

My spirit wearies of such blasphemy; and how such men can be supported as the "standing types and representatives of Jesus Christ" is a mystery which I leave others to penetrate. In speaking of the American church, however, let it be distinctly understood that I mean the *great mass* of the religious organizations of our land. There are exceptions, and I thank God that there are. Noble men may be found, scattered all over these Northern states, of whom Henry Ward Beecher, of Brooklyn; Samuel J. May, of Syracuse; and my esteemed friend [Rev. R. R. Raymond] on the platform, are shining examples; and let me say further, that upon these men lies the duty to inspire our ranks with high religious faith and zeal, and to cheer us on in the great mission of the slave's redemption from his chains.

One is struck with the difference between the attitude of the American church toward the antislavery movement and that occupied by the churches in England toward a similar movement in that country. There, the church, true to its mission of ameliorating, elevating and improving the condition of mankind, came forward promptly, bound up the wounds of the West Indian slave, and restored him to his liberty. There, the question of emancipation was a high religious question. It was demanded in the name of humanity and according to the law of the living God. The Sharps, the Clarksons, the Wilberforces, the Buxtons, the Burchells, and the Knibbs were alike famous for their piety and for their philanthropy. The antislavery movement *there* was not an antichurch movement, for the reason that the church took its full share in prosecuting that movement: and the antislavery movement in this country will cease to be an antichurch movement when the church of this country shall assume a favorable instead of a hostile position toward that movement.

Americans! your republican politics, not less than your republican religion, are flagrantly inconsistent. You boast of your love of liberty, your superior civilization and your pure Christianity, while the whole political power of the nation (as embodied in the two great political parties) is solemnly pledged to support and perpetuate the enslavement of three millions of your countrymen. You hurl your anathemas at the crowned-headed tyrants of Russia and Austria and pride yourselves on your democratic institutions, while you yourselves consent to be the mere *tools* and *bodyguards* of the tyrants of Virginia and Carolina. You invite to your shores fugitives of oppression from abroad, honor them with banquets, greet them with ovations, cheer them, toast them, salute them, protect them, and pour out your money to them like water; but the fugitives from your own land you advertise, hunt, arrest, shoot and kill. You glory in your refinement and your universal education; yet you maintain a system as barbarous and dreadful as ever stained the character of a nation—a system begun in avarice, supported in pride, and perpetuated in cruelty. You shed tears over fallen Hungary, and make the sad story of her wrongs the theme of your poets, statesmen and orators, till your gallant sons are ready to fly to arms to vindicate her cause against her oppressors; but, in regard to the ten thousand wrongs of the American slave, you would enforce the strictest silence and would hail him as an enemy of the nation who dares to make those wrongs the subject of public discourse! You are all on fire at the mention of liberty for France or for Ireland, but are as cold as an iceberg at the thought of liberty for the enslaved of America. You discourse eloquently on the dignity of labor; yet, you sustain a system which, in its very essence, casts a stigma upon labor. You can bare your bosom to the storm of British artillery to throw off a three-penny tax on tea, and yet wring the last hard-earned farthing from the grasp of the black laborers of your country. You profess to believe "that of one blood God made all nations of men to dwell on the face of all the earth" and hath commanded all men, everywhere, to love one another; yet you notoriously hate (and glory in your hatred) all men whose skins are not colored like your own. You declare before the world, and are understood by the world to declare, that you *"hold these truths to be self-evident, that all men are created equal; and are endowed by their Creator with certain inalienable rights; and that among these are, life, liberty and the pursuit of happiness"*; and yet, you hold securely, in a bondage which, according to your own Thomas Jefferson, *"is worse than ages of that which your fathers rose in rebellion to oppose," a seventh part* of the inhabitants of your country.

Fellow citizens, I will not enlarge further on your national inconsistencies. The existence of slavery in this country brands your republicanism as a sham, your humanity as a base pretence, and your Christianity as a lie. It destroys your moral power abroad; it corrupts your politicians at home. It saps the foundation of religion; it makes your name a hissing and a by word to a mocking earth. It is the antagonistic force in your government, the only thing that seriously disturbs and endangers your union. It fetters your progress; it is the enemy of improvement; the deadly foe of education; it fosters pride; it breeds insolence; it promotes vice; it shelters crime; it is a curse to the earth that supports it; and yet you cling to it as if it were the sheet anchor of all your hopes. Oh, be warned! Be warned! A horrible reptile is coiled up in your nation's bosom; the venomous creature is nursing at the tender breast of your youthful republic; *for the love of God, tear away,* and fling from you the hideous monster, and *let the weight of twenty millions crush and destroy it forever!*

But it is answered in reply to all this, that precisely what I have now denounced is, in fact, guaranteed and sanctioned by the Constitution of the United States, that the right to hold and to hunt slaves is a part of that Constitution framed by the illustrious Fathers of this Republic.

Then, I dare to affirm, notwithstanding all I have said before, your fathers stooped, basely stooped

> *To palter with us in a double sense:*
> *And keep the word of promise to the ear,*
> *But break it to the heart.*

And instead of being the honest men I have before declared them to be, they were the veriest imposters that ever practiced on mankind. This is the inevitable conclusion, and from it there is no escape; but I differ from those who charge this baseness on the framers of the Constitution of the United States. It is a slander upon their memory, at least, so I believe. There is not time now to argue the Constitutional question at length; nor have I the ability to discuss it as it ought to be discussed. The subject has been handled with masterly power by Lysander Spooner, Esq., by William Goodell, by Samuel E. Sewall, Esq., and last, though not least, by Gerrit Smith, Esq. These gentlemen have, as I think, fully and clearly vindicated the Constitution from any design to support slavery for an hour.

Fellow citizens, there is no matter in respect to which the people of the North have allowed themselves to be so ruinously imposed upon as that of the proslavery character of the Constitution. In that instrument I hold there is neither warrant, license nor sanction of the hateful thing; but, interpreted as it ought to be interpreted, the Constitution is a glorious liberty document. Read its preamble, consider its purposes. Is slavery among them? Is it at the gateway? Or is it in the temple? It is neither. While I do not intend to argue this question on the present occasion, let me ask, if it be not somewhat singular that, if the Constitution were intended to be, by its framers and adopters, a slaveholding instrument, why neither *slavery,* *slaveholding* nor *slave* can anywhere be found in it. What would be thought of an instrument, drawn up, legally drawn up, for the purpose of entitling the city of Rochester to a tract of land, in which no mention of land was made? Now, there are certain rules of interpretation for the proper understanding of all legal instruments. These rules are well established. They are plain, common-sense rules, such as you and I and all of us can understand and apply, without having passed years in the study of law. I scout the idea that the question of the constitutionality, or unconstitutionality of slavery, is not a question for the people. I hold that every American citizen has a right to form an opinion of the Constitution, and to propagate that opinion, and to use all honorable means to make his opinion the prevailing one. Without this right, the liberty of an American citizen would be as insecure as that of a Frenchman. Ex-Vice-President Dallas tells us that the Constitution is an object to which no American mind can be too attentive, and no American heart too devoted. He further says, the Constitution, in its words, is plain and intelligible, and is meant for the home-bred, unsophisticated understandings of our fellow citizens. Senator Berrien tells us that the Constitution is the fundamental law, that which controls all others. The charter of our liberties, which every citizen has a personal interest in understanding thoroughly. The testimony of Senator [Sidney] Breese, Lewis Cass, and many others that might be named, who are everywhere esteemed as sound lawyers, so regard the Constitution. I take it, therefore, that it is not presumption in a private citizen to form an opinion of that instrument.

Now, take the Constitution according to its plain reading, and I defy the presentation of a single proslavery clause in it. On the other hand, it will be found to contain principles and purposes, entirely hostile to the existence of slavery.

I have detained my audience entirely too long already. At some future period I will gladly avail myself of an opportunity to give this subject a full and fair discussion.

Allow me to say, in conclusion, notwithstanding the dark picture I have this day presented, of the state of the nation, I do not despair of this country. There are forces in operation which must inevitably work the downfall of slavery. "The arm of the Lord is not shortened," and the doom of slavery is certain. I, therefore, leave off where I began, with hope. While drawing encouragement from "the Declaration of Independence," the great principles it contains and the genius of American institutions, my spirit is also cheered by the obvious tendencies of the age. Nations do not now stand in the same relation to each other that they did ages ago. No nation can now shut itself up from the surrounding world and trot round in the same old path of its fathers without interference. The time was when such could be done. Long-established customs of hurtful character could formerly fence themselves in and do their evil work with social impunity. Knowledge was then confined and enjoyed by the privileged few, and the multitude walked on in mental darkness. But a change has now come over the affairs of mankind. Walled cities and empires have become unfashionable. The arm of commerce has borne away the gates of the strong city. Intelligence is penetrating the darkest corners of the globe. It makes its pathway over and under the sea, as well as on the earth. Wind, steam and lightning are its chartered agents. Oceans no longer divide, but link nations together. From Boston to London is now a holiday excursion. Space is comparatively annihilated. Thoughts expressed on one side of the Atlantic are distinctly heard on the other.

The far-off and almost fabulous Pacific rolls in grandeur at our feet. The Celestial Empire, the mystery of ages, is being solved. The fiat of the Almighty, "Let there be Light," has not yet spent its force. No abuse, no outrage, whether in taste, sport or avarice, can now hide itself from the all-pervading light. The iron shoe and crippled foot of China must be seen in contrast with nature. Africa must rise and put on her yet unwoven garment. "Ethiopia shall stretch out her hand unto God." In the fervent aspirations of William Lloyd Garrison, I say, and let every heart join in saying it,

> *God speed the year of jubilee*
> *The wide world o'er!*
> *When from their galling chains set free,*
> *Th' oppress'd shall vilely bend the knee,*
> *And wear the yoke of tyranny*
> *Like brutes no more.*
> *That year will come, and freedom's reign,*
> *To man his plundered rights again*
> *Restore.*

> *God speed the day when human blood*
> *Shall cease to flow!*
> *In every clime be understood,*
> *The claims of human brotherhood,*
> *And each return for evil, good,*
> *Not blow for blow;*
> *That day will come all feuds to end,*
> *And change into a faithful friend*
> *Each foe.*

God speed the hour, the glorious hour,
    When none on earth
Shall exercise a lordly power,
Nor in a tyrant's presence cower;
But all to manhood's stature tower,
    By equal birth!
That hour will come, to each, to all,
And from his prison-house, the thrall
    Go forth.

Until that year, day, hour, arrive
With head, and heart, and hand I'll strive,
To break the rod, and rend the gyve,
The spoiler of his prey deprive—
    So witness Heaven!
And never from my chosen post,
Whate'er the peril or the cost,
    Be driven.

John Sweat Rock

(1825–1866)

A DEEP AND CRUEL PREJUDICE

January 23, 1862

John Sweat Rock was born a free man in Salem, New Jersey, in 1825. One of the first African-American doctors in the United States, Rock practiced dentistry for over a decade, until his faltering health forced him to give up his practice. Upon leaving medicine, he studied law, passing the bar in Massachusetts in 1861. Rock was the first African American granted admittance to argue cases in front of the United States Supreme Court. The following speech was delivered before the Massachusetts Anti-Slavery Society.

LADIES AND GENTLEMEN: I am here not so much to make a speech as to add a little more *color* to this occasion. [Laughter.]

I do not know that it is right that I should speak, at this time, for it is said that we have talked too much already; and it is being continually thundered in our ears that the time for speech-making has ended, and the time for action has arrived. Perhaps this is so. This may be the theory of the people, but we all know that the active idea has found but little sympathy with either of our great military commanders, or the national Executive; for they have told us, again and again, that "patience is a cure for all sores," and that we must wait for the "good time," which, to us, has been long a-coming.

It is not my desire, neither is it the time for me to criticize the government, even if I had the disposition so to do. The situation of the black man in this country is far from being an enviable one. Today our heads are in the lion's mouth, and we must get them out the best way we can. To contend against the government is as difficult as it is to sit in Rome and fight with the Pope. It is probable that, if we had the malice of the Anglo-Saxon, we would watch our chances and seize the first opportunity to take our revenge. If we attempted this, the odds would be against us, and the first thing we should know would be—nothing! The most of us are capable of perceiving that he man who spits against the wind, spits in his own face! [Laughter.]

While Mr. Lincoln has been more conservative than I had hoped to find him, I recognize in him an honest man, striving to redeem the country from the degradation and shame into which Mr. Buchanan and his predecessors have plunged it.

This nation is mad. In its devoted attachment to the Negro, it has run crazy after him and now, having caught him, hangs on with a deadly grasp, and says to him, with more earnestness and pathos than Ruth expressed to Naomi, "Where thou goest, I will go; where thou lodgest, I will lodge; thy people shall be my people, and thy God my God."

Why this wonderful attachment? My brother (Mr. Remond) spoke ably and eloquently to you this afternoon, and told of you of the cruel and inhuman prejudices of the white people of this country. He was right. But has he not failed to look on the other side of this question? Has he not observed the deep and abiding affection that they have for the Negro, which "neither height, nor depth, nor principalities, nor powers, nor things present nor to come, can separate from this love," which reaches to their very souls? [Renewed laughter and applause.]

I do not deny that there is a deep and cruel prejudice lurking in the bosoms of the white people of this country. It is much more abundant in the North than in the South. Here, it is to be found chiefly among the higher and lower classes; and there is no scarcity of it among the poor whites at the South. The cause of this prejudice may be seen at a glance.

The educated and wealthy class despise the Negro, because they have robbed him of his hard earnings, or, at least, have got rich off the fruits of his labor; and they believe if he gets his freedom, their fountain will be dried up and they will be obliged to seek business in a new channel. Their "occupation will be gone." The lowest class hate him because he is poor, as they are, and he is a competitor with them for the same labor. The poor ignorant white man, who does not understand that the interest of the laboring classes is mutual, argues in this wise: "Here is so much labor to be performed. That Negro does it. If he was gone, I should have his place." The rich and the poor are both prejudiced from interest, and not because they entertain vague notions of justice and humanity. While uttering my solemn protest against this American vice, which has done more than any other thing to degrade the American people in the eyes of the civilized world, I am happy to state that there are many who have never known this sin, and many others who have been converted to the truth by the "foolishness of antislavery preaching," and are deeply interested in the welfare of the race and never hesitate to use their means and their influence to help break off the yoke that has been so long crushing us. I thank them all, and hope the number may be multiplied, until we shall have a people who will know no man save by his virtues and his merits.

Now, it seems to me that a blind man can see that the present war is an effort to nationalize, perpetuate and extend slavery in this country. In short, slavery is the cause of the war: I might say, is *the* war itself. Had it not been for slavery, we should have had no war! Through two hundred and forty years of indescribable tortures, slavery has wrung out of the blood, bones and muscles of the Negro hundreds of millions of dollars and helped much to make this nation rich. At the same time, it has developed a volcano which has burst forth, and, in a less number of days than years, has dissipated this wealth and rendered the government bankrupt! And, strange as it may appear, you still cling to this monstrous iniquity, notwithstanding it is daily sinking the country lower and lower! Some of our ablest and best men have been sacrificed to appease the wrath of this American god. There was Fremont—God bless him [loud applause]— who, under pretense of frauds in his contracts, to the amount of several thousand dollars, was set aside for a Hunker kidnapper. If Fremont made a mistake of a few thousand dollars,—which no one claims was intentional, on his part,—what do you think of the terrible delay which has cost, and is costing, us two millions a day? Who is responsible for this great sacrifice of treasure? [Hear, hear.] Then, there was Mr. Cameron, the hem of whose garment was not soiled with Anti-Slavery, except what he got from his official position, as it was forced upon his convictions. But, standing where he did, he saw the real enemy of the country; and because he favored striking at its vitals, his head was cut off, and that of a Hunker's substituted!

There is a storm in that cloud which, today, though no larger than a man's hand, is destined to sweep over this country and wake up this guilty nation. Then we shall know where the fault is, and if these dry bones can live! The government wishes us to bring back the country to what it was before. This is possible; but what is to be gained by it? If we are fools enough to retain the cancer that is eating out our vitals when we can safely extirpate it, who will pity us if we see our mistake when we are past recovery? The Abolitionists saw this day of tribulation and reign of terror long ago and warned you of it; *but you would not hear!* You now say that it is their agitation, which has brought about this terrible civil war! That is to say, your friend sees a slow match set near a keg of gunpowder in your house and timely warns you of the danger which he sees is inevitable; you despise his warning and, after the explosion, say if he had not told you of it it would not have happened!

Now, when some leading men who hold with the policy of the

President and yet pretend to be liberal argue that while they are willing to admit that the slave has an undoubted right to his liberty, the master has an equal right to his property; that to liberate the slave would be to injure the master, and a greater good would be accomplished to the country in these times by the loyal master's retaining his property than by giving to the slave his liberty—I do not understand it so. Slavery is treason against God, man and the nation. The master has no right to be a partner in a conspiracy which has shaken the very foundation of the government. Even to apologize for it, while in open rebellion, is to aid and abet in treason. The master's right to his property in human flesh cannot be equal to the slave's right to his liberty. The former right is acquired, either by kidnapping or unlawful purchase from kidnappers, or inheritance from kidnappers. The very claim invalidates itself. On the other hand, liberty is the inalienable right of every human being; and liberty can make no compromise with slavery. The goodness of slavery to the master can bear no relative comparison to the goodness of liberty to the slave. Liberty and slavery are contraries, and separated from each other as good from evil, light from darkness, heaven from hell. [Applause.] We trace effects to their cause. The evils brought upon the slave and the free colored man are traced to slavery. If slavery is better than freedom, its effects must also be better; for the better effect is from the better cause, and the better results from the better principle; and conversely, of better effects and results, the causes and principles are better. The greater good is that which we would most desire to be the cause to ourselves and our friends, and the greater evil is that which would give us the deeper affliction to have involved upon them or ourselves. Now, there is no sane man who would not rather have his liberty, and be stripped of every other earthly comfort, and see his friends in a like situation, than be doomed to slavery with its indescribable category of cruelty and wrongs—

> *"Sometimes loaded with heavy chains,*
> *and flogged till the keen lash stains."*

It may be an easy matter to apologize for slavery but after applying the great test,—the Golden Rule—of "doing unto others as we would have them do unto us," we must admit that no apology can be made for slavery. And of all the miserable miscreants who have attempted to apologize for, and extol, the happy condition of the slave, I have never seen one of them willing to take the place of one of these so-called "happy creatures." [Loud applause.]

Today, when it is a military necessity and when the safety of the country is dependent upon emancipation, our humane political philosophers are puzzled to know what would become of the slaves if they were emancipated! The idea seems to prevail that the poor things would suffer if robbed of the glorious privileges they now enjoy! If they could not be flogged, half-starved, and work to support in ease and luxury those who have never waived an opportunity to outrage and wrong them, they would pine away and die! Do you imagine that the Negro can live outside of slavery? Of course, now they can take care of themselves and their masters too; but if you give them their liberty, must they not suffer? Have you never been able to see through all this? Have you not observed that the location of this organ of sympathy is in the pocket of the slaveholder and the man who shares in the profits of slave labor? Of course you have; and pity those men who have lived upon their ill-gotten wealth. You know, if they do not have somebody to work for them, they must leave their gilded *salons* and take off their coats and roll up their sleeves and take their chances among the *live* men of the world. This, you are aware, these respectable gentlemen will not do, for they have been so long accustomed to live by robbing and cheating the Negro that they are sworn never to work while they can live by plunder.

Can the slaves take care of themselves? What do you suppose becomes of the thousands who fly ragged and penniless from the South every year, and scatter themselves throughout the free states of the North? Do they take care of themselves? I am neither ashamed nor afraid to meet this question. Assertions like this, long uncontradicted, seem to be admitted as established facts. I ask your attention for one moment to the fact that colored men at the North are shut out of almost every avenue to wealth, and yet, strange to say, the proportion of paupers is much less among us than among you! Are the beggars in the streets of Boston colored men? In Philadelphia, where there is a larger free colored population than is to be found in any other city in the free states, and where we are denied every social privilege and are not even permitted to send our children to the schools that we are taxed to support or to ride in the city horsecars, yet even there we pay taxes enough to support our own poor, and have a balance of a few thousand in our favor, pressed and enslaved! Another reason is, this nation has wronged us and for this reason many hate us. The Spanish proverb is—"since I have wronged you, I have never liked you." This is true not only of Spaniards and Americans, but of every other class of people. When a man wrongs another, he not only hates him, but tries to make others dislike him. Strange as this may appear, it is nevertheless painfully true. You may help a man during his lifetime, and you are a capital fellow; but your first refusal brings down his ire, and shows you his ingratitude. When he has got all he can from you, he has no further use for you. When the orange is squeezed, we throw it aside. The black man is a good fellow while he is a slave and toils for nothing; but the moment he claims his own flesh and blood and bones he is a most obnoxious creature, and there is a proposition to get rid of him! He is happy while he remains a poor, degraded, ignorant slave, without even the right to his own offspring. While in this condition, the master can ride in the same carriage, sleep in the same bed, and nurse from the same bosom. But give this same slave the right to use his own legs, his hands, his body and his mind, and this happy and desirable creature is instantly transformed into a miserable loathsome wretch, fit only to be colonized somewhere near the mountains of the moon, or eternally banished from the presence of all civilized beings. You must not lose sight of the fact that it is the emancipated slave and the free colored man whom it is proposed to remove—not the slave; this country and climate are perfectly adapted to Negro slavery; it is the free black that the air is not good for! What an idea! A country good for slavery, and not good for freedom! This idea is monstrous and unworthy of even the Fejee islanders. All the Emigration and Colonization Societies that have been formed, have been auxiliaries of the Slave Power, and established for this purpose, and the great desire to make money out of our necessities. [Loud applause.]

It is true, a great many simple minded people have been induced to go to Liberia and to Hayti, but, be assured, the more intelligent portion of the colored people will remain here; not because we prefer being oppressed here to being free men in other countries, but we will remain because we believe our future prospects are better here than elsewhere, and because our experience has proved that the greater proportion of those who have left this country during the last thirty years have made their condition worse, and would have gladly returned if they could have done so. You may rest assured that we shall remain here—here, where we have withstood almost everything. Now, when our prospects begin to brighten, we are the more encouraged to stay, pay off the old score and have a reconstruction of things. There are those of us who believe that we have seen the star of our redemption rising in the east, and moving southward. [Applause.]

The government is now trying to untie the knot which must be cut. Here you perceive it is mistaken. The North is in error. She has suffered the South, like a wayward child, to do as she would, and now, when she would restrain her, she finds trouble. If you wish to prevent a pending evil, destroy the source at once. If the first sparks were quenched, there would be no flame, for how can he kill who dares not be angry? or how can he be perjured who fears an oath? All public outrages of a destroying tendency and oppression are but childish sports let alone till they are ungovernable. The choking of the fountain is the surest way to cut off the source of the river. The Government has not had the courage to do this. Having sown the wind, they are now reaping the whirlwind: but in the end I think it will be conceded by all, that we shall have gathered in a glorious harvest. [Loud applause.]

I do not regard this trying hour as a darkness. The war that has been waged on us for more than two centuries has opened our eyes and caused us to form alliances, so that instead of acting on the defensive we are now prepared to attack the enemy. This is simply a change of tactics. I think I see the finger of God in all this. Yes, *there* is the handwriting on the wall: *I come not to bring peace, but the sword. Break every yoke, and let the oppressed go free. I have heard the groans of my people and am come down to deliver them!* [Loud and long-continued applause.]

At present, it looks as though we were drafting into a foreign war; and if we do have one, slavery must go down with it. It is not the time now for me to discuss the relation of the black man to such a war. Perhaps no one cares what we think or how we feel on this subject. You think yourselves strong now. The wisest man and the strongest man is generally the most ignorant and the most feeble. Be not deceived. No man is so feeble that he cannot do you an injury! [Hear, hear.] If you should get into a difficulty of this kind, it would be to your interest that we should be your friends. You remember the lion had need of the mouse. [Applause.] You have spurned our offers, and disregarded our feelings, and on this account we have manifested but little interest in, and have been apparently indifferent observers of this contest; but appearances are deceitful—every man who snores is not asleep. [Applause.]

I believe the conduct of both the bond and the free has been exceedingly judicious. It is times like these that try men. It is storms and tempests that give reputation to pilots. If we have a foreign war, the black man's services will be needed. Seventy-five thousand freemen capable of bearing arms, and three-quarters of a million of slaves wild with the enthusiasm caused by the dawn of the glorious opportunity of being able to strike a genuine blow for freedom, will be a power that "white men will be bound to respect." [Applause.] Let the people of the United States do their duty, and treat us as the people of all other nations treat us—as men; if they will do this, our last drop of blood is ready to be sacrificed in defence of the liberty of this country. [Loud applause.] But if you continue to deny us our rights, and spurn our offers except as menials, colored men will be worse than fools to take up arms at all. [Hear, hear.] We will stand by you, however, and wish you that success which you will not deserve. [Applause.]

This rebellion for slavery means something! Out of it emancipation must spring. I do not agree with those men who see no hope in this war. There is nothing in it but hope. Our cause is onward. As it is with the sun, the clouds often obstruct his vision, but in the end we find there has been no standing still. It is true the government is but little more anti-slavery now than it was at the commencement of the war; but while fighting for its own existence, it has been obliged to take slavery by the throat, and sooner or later *must* choke her to death. [Loud applause.] Jeff Davis is to the slaveholders what Pharaoh was to the Egyptians, and Abraham Lincoln and his successor, John C. Fremont [Applause.], will be to us what Moses was to the Israelites. [Continued applause.] I may be mistaken, but I think the sequel will prove that I am correct. I have faith in God and gun-powder and lead, [Loud applause.] and believe we ought not to be discouraged. [Applause.] We have withstood the sixth trial, and in the seventh our courage must not falter. I thank God I have lived to see this great day, when the nation is to be weighed ion the balances, and I hope not found wanting. [Applause.] This State and the National Government have treated us most shamefully, but as this is not the first time, I suppose we shall live through it. In the hour of danger, we have not been found wanting. As the Government has not had the courage to receive the help that has been standing ready and waiting to assist her, we will now stand still, and see the salvation of our people. [Applause.]

John Mercer Langston

(1829–1897)

EQUALITY BEFORE THE LAW

May 17, 1874

The son of a wealthy slaveholder and a slave woman, John Mercer Langston was born into slavery in Virginia in 1829. After being emancipated upon the death of his father, Langston was educated at Oberlin College. He was the first African American elected to public office, as the township clerk of Brownhelm, Ohio. The following speech was delivered by Langston at his alma mater, Oberlin College; the occasion was the celebration of the anniversary of the adoption of the Fifteenth Amendment.

MR. PRESIDENT AND FRIENDS: I thank you for the invitation which brings me before you at this time, to address you upon this most interesting occasion. I am not unmindful of the fact that I stand in the presence of instructors, eminently distinguished for the work which they have done in the cause of truth and humanity. Oberlin was a pioneer in the labor of abolition. It is foremost in the work of bringing about equality of the Negro before the law. Thirty years ago on the first day of last March, it was my good fortune, a boy seeking an education, to see Oberlin for the first time. Here I discovered at once that I breathed a new atmosphere. Though poor, and a colored boy, I found no distinction made against me in your hotel, in your institution of learning, in your family circle. I come here today with a heart full of gratitude to say to you in this public way that I not only thank you for what you did for me individually, but for what you did for the cause whose success makes this day the colored American a citizen sustained in all the rights, privileges and immunities of American citizenship.

As our country advances in civilization, prosperity and happiness, cultivating things which appertain to literature, science and law, may your

43

Oberlin, as in the past, so in all the future, go forward, cultivating a noble, patriotic, Christian leadership. In the name of the Negro, so largely blest and benefited by your institution, I bid you a hearty Godspeed.

Mr. President, within less than a quarter of a century, within the last fifteen years, the colored American has been raised from the condition of four-footed beasts and creeping things to the level of enfranchised manhood. Within this period the slave oligarchy of the land has been overthrown, and the nation itself emancipated from its barbarous rule. The compromise measures of 1850, including the Fugitive Slave law, together with the whole body of law enacted in the interest of slavery, then accepted as finalities, and the power of leading political parties pledged to their maintenance have, with those parties, been utterly nullified and destroyed. In their stead we have a purified Constitution and legislation no longer construed and enforced to sanction and support inhumanity and crime, but to sustain and perpetuate the freedom and the rights of us all.

Indeed, two nations have been born in a day. For in the death of slavery, and through the change indicated, the colored American has been spoken into the new life of liberty and law; while new, other and better purposes, aspirations and feelings have possessed and moved the soul of his fellow countrymen. The moral atmosphere of the land is no longer that of slavery and hate; as far as the late slave, even, is concerned, it is largely that of freedom and fraternal appreciation.

Not forgetting the struggle and sacrifice of the people, the matchless courage and endurance of our soldiery, necessary to the salvation of the Government and Union, our freedom and that reconstruction of sentiment and law essential to their support, it is eminently proper that we all leave our ordinary callings this day, to join in cordial commemoration of our emancipation, the triumph of a movement whose comprehensive results profit and bless without discrimination as to color or race.

Hon. Benjamin F. Butler, on the 4th day of July last, in addressing his fellow citizens of Massachusetts, at Framingham, used the following language, as I conceive, with propriety and truth:

> "But another and, it may not be too much to say, greater event has arisen within this generation. The rebellion sought to undo all that '76 had done, and to dissolve the nation then born, and to set aside the Declaration that all men are created equal, with certain inalienable rights, among which are life, liberty and the pursuit of happiness. The war that ensued in suppressing this treasonable design, demanded so much greater effort, so much more terrible sacrifice, and has imprinted itself upon the people with so much more sharpness and freshness, that we of the present, and still more they of the coming

generation, almost forgetting '76, will remember '61 and '65, and the wrongs inflicted upon our fathers by King George and his ministers will be obliterated by the remembrance of the Proclamation of Emancipation, the assassination of the President, the restoration of the Union, and the reconstruction of the country in one united, and as we fondly trust, never to be dissevered nation."

The laws of a nation are no more the indices of its public sentiment and its civilization, than of its promise of progress toward the permanent establishment of freedom and equal rights. The histories of the empires of the past, no less than the nations of the present, bear testimony to the truthfulness of this statement. Because this is so, her laws, no less than her literature and science, constitute the glory of a nation, and render her influence lasting. This is particularly illustrated in the case of Rome, immortalized, certainly, not less by her laws than her letters or her arms. Hence, the sages, the jurists, and the statesmen of all ages, since Justinian, have dwelt with delight and admiration upon the excellences and beauties of Roman jurisprudence. Of the civil law Chancellor Kent eloquently says: "It was created and matured on the banks of the Tiber, by the successive wisdom of Roman statesmen, magistrates and sages; and after governing the greatest people in the ancient world for the space of thirteen or fourteen centuries, and undergoing extraordinary vicissitudes after the fall of the Western Empire, it was revived, admired and studied in northern Europe, on account of the variety and excellence of its general principles. It is now taught and obeyed not only in France, Spain, Germany, Holland, and Scotland, but in the islands of the Indian Ocean and on the banks of the Mississippi and the St. Lawrence. So true, it seems, are the words of d'Augesseau, that "the grand destinies of Rome are not yet accomplished; she reigns throughout the world by her reason, after having ceased to reign by her authority." And the reason through which she here reigns, is the reason of the law.

It is no more interesting to the patriot than to the philanthropist to trace the changes which have been made during the last decade in our legislation and law. Nor is there anything in these changes to cause regret or fear to the wise and sagacious lawyer or statesman. This is particularly true since, in the changes made, we essay no novel experiments in legislation and law, but such as are justified by principles drawn from the fountains of our jurisprudence, the Roman civil and the common law. It has been truthfully stated that the common law has made no distinction on account of race or color. None is now made in England or in any other Christian country of Europe. Nor is there any such distinction made, to my knowledge in the whole body of the Roman civil law.

Among the changes that have been wrought in the law of our coun-

try, in the order of importance and dignity, I would mention, first, that
slavery abolished, not by State but national enactment, can never again in
the history of our country be justified or defended on the ground that it
is a municipal institution, the creature of State law. Henceforth, as our
emancipation has been decreed by national declaration, our freedom is
shielded and protected by the strong arm of national law. Go where we
may, now, like the atmosphere about us, law protects us in our locomotion, our utterance, and our pursuit of happiness. And to this leading and
fundamental fact of the law the people and the various States of the
Union are adjusting themselves with grace and wisdom. It would be difficult to find a sane man in our country who would seriously advocate
the abrogation of the 13th amendment to the Constitution.

In our emancipation it is fixed by law that the place where we are born
is *ipso facto* our country; and this gives us a domicile, a home. As in slavery
we had no self ownership, nor interest in anything external to ourselves, so
we were without country and legal settlement. While slavery existed, even
the free colored American was in no better condition; and hence exhortations, prompted in many instances by considerations of philanthropy and
good-will, were not infrequently made to him to leave his native land, to
seek residence and home elsewhere, in distant and inhospitable regions.
These exhortations did not always pass unheeded; for eventually a national
organization was formed, having for its sole purpose the transportation to
Africa of such colored men as might desire to leave the land of their birth
to find settlement in that country. And through the influence of the
African Colonization Society not a few, even, of our most energetic, enter-
prising, industrious and able colored men, not to mention thousands of the
humbler class, have been carried abroad.

It may be that, in the providence of God, these persons, self-expatriated,
may have been instrumental in building up a respectable and promising
government in Liberia, and that those who have supported the Colonization
Society have been philanthropically disposed, both as regards the class
transported and the native African. It is still true, however, that the emancipated American has hitherto been driven or compelled to consent to
expatriation because denied legal home and settlement in the land of his
nativity. Expatriation is no longer thus compelled; for it is now settled
in the law, with respect to the colored, as well as all other native-born
Americans, that the country of his birth, even this beautiful and goodly
land, is his country. Nothing, therefore, appertaining to it, its rich and
inexhaustible resources, its industry and commerce, its education and
religion, its law and Government, the glory and perpetuity of its free
institutions and Union, can be without lively and permanent interest to
him, as to all others who, either by birth or adoption, legitimately claim
it as their country.

With emancipation, then, comes also that which is dearer to the true patriot than life itself: country and home. And this doctrine of the law, in the broad and comprehensive application explained, is now accepted without serious objection by leading jurists and statesmen.

The law has also forever determined, and to our advantage, that nativity, without any regard to nationality or complexion, settles, absolutely, the question of citizenship. One can hardly understand how citizenship, predicated upon birth, could have ever found place among the vexed questions of the law; certainly American law. We have only to read, however, the official opinions given by leading and representative American lawyers, in slaveholding times, to gain full knowledge to the existence of this fact. According to these opinions our color, race and degradation, all or either, rendered the colored American incapable of being or becoming a citizen of the United States. As early as November 7th, 1821, during the official term of President Monroe, the Hon. William Wirt, of Virginia, then acting as Attorney-General of the United States, in answer to the question propounded by the Secretary of the Treasury, "whether free persons of color are, in Virginia, citizens of the United States within the intent and meaning of the acts regulating foreign and coasting trade, so as to be qualified to command vessels," replied, saying among other things: "Free Negroes and mulattoes can satisfy the requisitions of age and residence as well as the white man; and if nativity, residence and allegiance combined (without the rights and privileges of a white man) are sufficient to make him a citizen of the United States, in the sense of the Constitution, then free Negroes and mulattoes are eligible to those high offices," (of President, Senator or Representative,) "and may command the purse and sword of the nation." After able and elaborate argument to show that nativity in the case of the colored American does not give citizenship, according to the meaning of the Constitution of the United States, Mr. Wirt concludes his opinion in these words: "Upon the whole, I am of the opinion that free persons of color, in Virginia, are not citizens of the United States, within the intent and meaning of the acts regulating foreign and coasting trade, so as to be qualified to command vessels."

This subject was further discussed in 1843, when the Hon. John C. Spencer, then Secretary of the Treasury, submitted to Hon. H. S. Legare, Attorney-General of the United States, in behalf of the Commissioner of the General Land Office, with request that his opinion be given thereon, "whether a free man of color, in the case presented, can be admitted to the privileges of a pre-emptioner under the act of September 4, 1841." In answering this question, Mr. Legare held: "It is not necessary, in my view of the matter, to discuss the question how far a free man of color may be a citizen in the highest sense of that word that is, one who enjoys in the fullest manner all the *jura civitatis* under the Constitution of the

United States. It is the plain meaning of the act to give the right of pre-emption to all denizens; any foreigner who had filed his declaration of intention to become a citizen is rendered at once capable of holding land." Continuing, he says: "Now, free people of color are not aliens, they enjoy universally (while there has been no express statutory provision to the contrary) the rights of denizens."

This opinion of the learned Attorney-General, while it admits the free man of color to the privileges of a pre-emptioner under the act mentioned, places him legally in a nondescript condition, erroneously assuming, as we clearly undertake to say, that there are degrees and grades of American citizenship. These opinions accord well with the *dicta* of the Dred-Scott decision, of which we have lively remembrance.

But a change was wrought in the feeling and conviction of our country, as indicated in the election of Abraham Lincoln President of the United States. On the 22nd day of September, 1862, he issued his preliminary Emancipation Proclamation. On the 29th day of the following November Salmon P. Chase, then Secretary of the Treasury, propounded to Edward Bates, then Attorney-General, the same question in substance which had been put in 1821 to William Wirt, viz.: "Are colored men citizens of the United States, and therefore competent to command American vessels?" The reasoning and the conclusion reached by Edward Bates were entirely different from that of his predecessor, William Wirt. Nor does Edward Bates leave the colored American in the anomalous condition of a "denizen." In his masterly and exhaustive opinion, creditable alike to his ability and learning, his patriotism and philanthropy, he maintains that "free men of color, if born in the United States, are citizens of the United States; and, if otherwise qualified, are competent, according to the acts of Congress, to be masters of vessels engaged in the coasting trade. In the course of his argument he says:

1. "In every civilized country the individual is born to duties and rights, the duty of allegiance and the right to protection, and these are correlative obligations, the one the price of the other, and they constitute the all-sufficient bond of union between the individual and his country, and the country he is born in is *prima facie* his country.

2. "And our Constitution, in speaking of natural-born citizens, uses no affirmative language to make them such, but only recognizes and reaffirms the universal principle, common to all nations and as old as political society, that the people born in the country do constitute the nation, and, as individuals, are natural members of the body politic.

3. "In the United States it is too late to deny the political rights and obligations conferred and imposed by nativity; for our laws do not pretend to create or enact them, but do assume and recognize them

as things known to all men, because pre-existent and natural, and, therefore, things of which the laws must take cognizance.

4. "It is strenuously insisted by some that 'persons of color,' though born in the country, are not capable of being citizens of the United States. As far as the Constitution is concerned, this is a naked assumption, for the Constitution contains not one word upon the subject.

5. "There are some who, abandoning the untenable objection of color, still contend that no person descended from Negroes of the African race can be a citizen of the United States. Here the objection is not color but race only. ★ ★ ★ ★ The Constitution certainly does not forbid it, but is silent about race as it is about color.

6. "But it is said that African Negroes are a degraded race, and that all who are tainted with that degradation are forever disqualified for the functions of citizenship. I can hardly comprehend the thought of the absolute incompatibility of degradation and citizenship; I thought that they often went together.

7. "Our nationality was created and our political government exists by written law, and inasmuch as that law does not exclude persons of that descent, and as its terms are manifestly broad enough to include them, it follows, inevitably, that such persons born in the country must be citizens unless the fact of African descent be so incompatible with the fact of citizenship that the two cannot exist together."

When it is recollected that these broad propositions with regard to citizenship predicated upon nativity, and in the case of free colored men, were enunciated prior to the first day of January, 1863, before emancipation, before even the 13th amendment of the Constitution was adopted; when the law stood precisely as it was, when Wirt and Legare gave their opinions, it must be conceded that Bates was not only thoroughly read in the law, but bold and sagacious. For these propositions have all passed, through the 14th amendment, into the Constitution of the United States, and are sustained by a wise and well-defined public judgment.

With freedom decreed by law, citizenship sanctioned and sustained thereby, the duty of allegiance on the one part, and the right of protection on the other recognized and enforced, even if considerations of political necessity had not intervened, the gift of the ballot to the colored American could not have long been delayed. The 15th amendment is the logical and legal consequence of the 13th and 14th amendments of the Constitution. Considerations of political necessity, as indicated, no doubt hastened the adoption of this amendment. But in the progress of legal development in our country, consequent upon the triumph of the abolition movement, its coming was inevitable. And, therefore, as its legal necessity, as well as political, is recognized and admitted, opposition to it has well-nigh disappeared. Indeed, so far from there being anything like general and organized opposition to the exercise of political powers by the enfranchised American, the people accept it as a fit and natural fact.

Great as the change has been with regard to the legal status of the colored American, in his freedom, his enfranchisement, and the exercise of political powers, he is not yet given the full exercise and enjoyment of all the rights which appertain by law to American citizenship. Such as are still denied him are withheld on the plea that their recognition would result in social equality, and his demand for them is met by considerations derived from individual and domestic opposition. Such reasoning is no more destitute of logic than law. While I hold that opinion sound which does not accept mere prejudice and caprice instead of the promptings of nature, guided by cultivated taste and wise judgment as the true basis of social recognition; and believing, too, that in a Christian community, social recognition may justly be pronounced a duty, I would not deal in this discussion with matters of society. I would justify the claim of the colored American to complete equality of rights and privileges upon well considered and accepted principles of law.

As showing the condition and treatment of the colored citizens of this country, anterior to the introduction of the Civil Rights Bill, so called, into the United States Senate, by the late Hon. Charles Sumner, I ask your attention to the following words from a letter written by him:

"I wish a bill carefully drawn, supplementary to the existing Civil Rights Law, by which all citizens shall be protected in equal rights:—

"1. On railroads, steamboats and public conveyances, being public carriers.
"2. At all houses in the nature of 'inns.'
"3. All licensed houses of public amusement.
"4. At all common schools.

"Can you do this? I would follow as much as possible the language of the existing Civil Rights Law, and make the new bill supplementary."

It will be seen from this very clear and definite statement of the Senator, that in his judgment, in spite of and contrary to common law rules applied in the case, certainly of all others, and recognized as fully settled, the colored citizen was denied those accommodations, facilities, advantages and privileges, furnished ordinarily by common carriers, innkeepers, at public places of amusement and common schools; and which are so indispensable to rational and useful enjoyment of life, that without them citizenship itself loses much of its value, and liberty seems little more than a name.

The judicial axiom, *"omnes homines oequales sunt,"* is said to have been given the world by the jurisconsults of the Antonine era. From the Roman, the French people inherited this legal sentiment; and, through the learning, the wisdom and patriotism of Thomas Jefferson and his Revolutionary compatriots, it was made the chief corner-stone of jurisprudence and politics. In considering the injustice done the colored American in denying him common school advantages, on general and equal terms with all others, impartial treatment in the conveyances of common carriers, by sea and land, and the enjoyment of the usual accommodations afforded travelers at public inns, and in vindicating his claim to the same, it is well to bear in mind this fundamental and immutable principle upon which the fathers built, and in the light of which our law ought to be construed and enforced. This observation has especial significance as regards the obligations and liabilities of common carriers and inn-keepers; for from the civil law we have borrowed those principles largely which have controlling force in respect to these subjects. It is manifest, in view of this statement, that the law with regard to these topics is neither novel nor unsettled; and when the colored American asks its due enforcement in his behalf, he makes no unnatural and strange demand.

Denied, generally, equal school advantages, the colored citizen demands them in the name of that equality of rights and privileges which is the vital element of American law. Equal in freedom, sustained by law; equal in citizenship, defined and supported by the law; equal in the exercise of political powers, regulated and sanctioned by law; by what refinement of reasoning, or tenet of law, can the denial of common school and other educational advantages be justified? To answer, that so readeth the statute, is only to drive us back of the letter to the reasonableness, the soul of the law, in the name of which we would, as we do, demand the repeal of that enactment which is not only not law, but contrary to its simplest requirements. It may be true that that which ought to be law is not always so written; but, in this matter, that only ought to remain upon the statute book, to be enforced as to citizens and voters, which is law in the truest and best sense.

Without dwelling upon the advantages of a thorough common school education, I will content myself by offering several considerations against the proscriptive, and in favor of the common school. A common school should be one to which all citizens may send their children, not by favor, but by right. It is established and supported by the Government; its criterion is a public foundation; and one citizen has as rightful claim upon its privileges and advantages as any other. The money set apart to its organization and support, whatever the sources whence it is drawn, whether from taxation or appropriation, having been dedicated to the public use, belongs as much to one as to another citizen; and no principle of law can be adduced to justify any arbitrary classification which excludes the child of any citizen or class of citizens from equal enjoyment of the advantages purchased by such fund, it being the common property of every citizen equally, by reason of its public dedication.

Schools which tend to separate the children of the country in their feelings, aspirations and purposes, which foster and perpetuate sentiments of caste, hatred, and ill-will, which breed a sense of degradation on the one part and of superiority on the other, which beget clannish notions rather than teach and impress an omnipresent and living principle and faith that we are all Americans, in no wise realize our ideal of common schools, while they are contrary to the spirit of our laws and institutions.

Two separate school systems, tolerating discriminations in favor of one class against another, inflating on the one part, degrading on the other; two separate school systems, I say, tolerating such state of feeling and sentiment on the part of the classes instructed respectively in accordance therewith, cannot educate these classes to live harmoniously together, meeting the responsibilities and discharging the duties imposed by a common government in the interest of a common country.

The object of the common school is two-fold. In the first place it should bring to every child, especially the poor child, a reasonable degree of elementary education. In the second place it should furnish a common education, one similar and equal to all pupils attending it. Thus furnished, our sons enter upon business or professional walks with an equal start in life. Such education the Government owes to all classes of the people.

The obligations and liabilities of the common carrier of passengers can, in no sense, be made dependent upon the nationality or color of those with whom he deals. He may not, according to law, answer his engagements to one class and justify non-performance or neglect as to another by considerations drawn from race. His contract is originally and fundamentally with the entire community, and with all its members he is held to equal and impartial obligation. On this subject the rules of law are definite, clear, and satisfactory. These rules may be stated concisely as follows: It is the duty of the common carrier of passengers to receive all persons applying and who do not refuse to obey any reasonable regulations imposed, who are not guilty of gross and vulgar habits of conduct, whose characters are not doubtful, dissolute or suspicious or unequivocally bad, and whose object in seeking conveyance is not to interfere with the interests or patronage of the carrier so as to make his business less lucrative.

And, in the second place, common carriers may not impose upon passengers oppressive and grossly unreasonable orders and regulations. Were there doubt in regard to the obligation of common carriers as indicated, the authorities are abundant and might be quoted at large. Here, however, I need not make quotations. The only question which can arise as between myself and any intelligent lawyer, is as to whether the regulation made by common carriers of passengers generally in this country, by which passengers and colored ones are separated on steamboats, railroad cars, and stage coaches, greatly to the disadvantage, inconvenience, and dissatisfaction of the latter class, is reasonable. As to this question, I leave such lawyer to the books and his own conscience. We have advanced so far on this subject, in thought, feeling, and purpose, that the day cannot be distant when there will be found among us no one to justify such regulations by common carriers, and when they will be made to adjust themselves, in their orders and regulations with regard thereto to the rules of the common law. The grievance of the citizen in this particular is neither imaginary nor sentimental. His experience of sadness and pain attests its reality, and the awakening sense of the people generally, as discovered in their expressions, the decisions of several of our courts, and the recent legislation of a few States, shows that this particular discrimination, inequitable as it is illegal, cannot long be tolerated in any section of our country.

The law with regard to inn-keepers is not less explicit and rigid. They are not allowed to accommodate or refuse to accommodate wayfaring persons according to their own foolish prejudices or the senseless and cruel hatred of their guests.

Their duties are defined in the following language, the very words of the law:

> "Inns were allowed for the benefit of travelers, who have certain privileges whilst they are in their journeys, and are in a more peculiar manner protected by law.
>
> "If one who keeps a common inn refuses to receive a traveler as a guest into his house, or to find him victuals or lodging upon his tendering a reasonable price for the same, the inn-keeper is liable to render damages in an action at the suit of the party grieved, and may also be indicted and fined at the suit of the King.
>
> "An inn-keeper is not, if he has suitable room, at liberty to refuse to receive a guest who is ready and able to pay him a suitable compensation. On the contrary, he is bound to receive him, and if, upon false pretences, he refuses, he is liable to an action."

These are doctrines as old as the common law itself; indeed, older, for they come down to us from Gaius and Papinian. All discriminations made, therefore, by the keepers of public houses in the nature of inns, to the disadvantage, of the colored citizen, and contrary to the usual treatment accorded travelers, is not only wrong morally, but utterly illegal. To this judgment the public mind must soon come.

Had I the time, and were it not too great a trespass upon your patience, I should be glad to speak of the injustice and illegality, as well as inhumanity, of our exclusion, in some localities, from jury, public places of learning and amusement, the church and the cemetery. I will only say, however, (and in this statement I claim the instincts, not less than the well-formed judgment of mankind, in our behalf,) that such exclusion at least seems remarkable, and is difficult of defense upon any considerations of humanity, law, or Christianity. Such exclusion is the more remarkable and indefensible since we are fellow citizens, wielding like political powers, eligible to the same high official positions, responsible to the same degree and in the same manner for the discharge of the duties they impose; interested in the progress and civilization of a common country, and anxious, like all others, that its destiny be glorious and matchless. It is strange, indeed, that the colored American may find place in the Senate, but it is denied access and welcome to the public place of learning, the theatre, the church and the graveyard, upon terms accorded to all others.

But, Mr. President and friends, it ill becomes us to complain; we may not tarry to find fault. The change in public sentiment, the reform in our national legislation and jurisprudence, which we this day commemorate, transcendent and admirable, augurs and guarantees to all American citizens complete equality before the law, in the protection and enjoyment of all those rights and privileges which pertain to manhood, enfranchised and dignified. To us the 13th amendment of our Constitution, abolishing slavery and perpetuating freedom; the 14th amendment establishing citizenship and prohibiting the enactment of any law which shall abridge the privileges or immunities of citizens of the United States, or which shall deny the equal protection of the laws to all American citizens; and the 15th amendment, which declares that the RIGHT of citizens of the United States to vote shall not be denied or abridged by the United States or by any State, on account of race, color, or previous condition of servitude, are national utterances which only recognize, but sustain and perpetuate our freedom and rights.

To the colored American, more than to all others, the language of these amendments is not vain. To use the language of the late Hon. Charles Sumner, "within the sphere of their influence no person can be *created,* no person can be *born,* with civil or political privileges not enjoyed equally by all his fellow citizens; nor can any institution be established recognizing distinction of birth. Here is the great charter of every human being, drawing vital breath upon this soil, whatever may be his condition and whoever may be his parents. He may be poor, weak, humble or black; he may be of Caucasian, Jewish, Indian or Ethiopian race; he may be of French, German, English or Irish extraction; but before the Constitution all these distinctions disappear. He is not poor, weak, humble or black; nor is he Caucasian, Jew, Indian or Ethiopian; nor is he French, German, English or Irish—he is a *man,* the equal of all his fellow-men. He is one of the children of the State, which like an impartial parent, regards all its offspring with an equal care. To some it may justly allot higher duties according to higher capacities; but it welcomes all to its equal hospitable board. The State, imitating the Divine Justice, is no respecter of persons."

With freedom established in our own country, and equality before the law promised in early Federal, if not State legislation, we may well consider our duty with regard to the abolition of slavery, the establishment of freedom and free institutions upon the American continent, especially in the island of the seas, where slavery is maintained by despotic Spanish rule, and where the people declaring slavery abolished, and appealing to the civilized world for sympathy and justification of their course, have staked all upon "the dread arbitrament of war." There can be no peace on our continent, there can be no harmony among its people till slavery is everywhere abolished and freedom established and protected by law; the people themselves, making for themselves, and supporting their own government. Every nation, whether its home be an island or upon a continent, if oppressed, ought to have, like our own, a "new birth of freedom," and its "government of the people, by the people, and for the people," shall prove at once its strength and support.

Our sympathies especially go out towards the struggling patriots of Cuba. We would see the "Queen of the Antilles" free from Spanish rule; her slaves all freemen, and herself advancing in her freedom, across the way of national greatness and renown. Or if her million and a half inhabitants, with their thousands of rich and fertile fields, are unable to support national independence and unity, let her not look for protection from, or annexation to, a country and government despotic and oppressive in its policy. By its proximity to our shores, by the ties of blood which connect its population and ours; by the examples presented in our Revolutionary conflict, when France furnished succor and aid to our struggling but heroic fathers; by the lessons and examples of international law and history; by all the pledges made by our nation in favor of freedom and equal rights, the oppressed and suffering people of Cuba may justly expect, demand our sympathies and support in their struggle for freedom and independence. Especially let the colored American realize that where battle is made against despotism and oppression, wherever humanity struggles for national existence and recognition, there his sympathies should be felt, his word and succor inspiriting, encouraging and supporting. To-day let us send our word of sympathy to the struggling thousands of Cuba, among whom, as well as among the people of Porto Rico, we hope soon to see slavery, indeed, abolished, free institutions firmly established, and good order, prosperity and happiness secured. This accomplished, our continent is dedicated to freedom and free institutions; and the nations which compose its population will enjoy sure promise of national greatness and glory. Freedom and free institutions should be as broad as our continent. Among no nation here should there be found any enslaved or oppressed. "Compromises between right and wrong, under pretence of expediency," should disappear forever; our house should be no longer divided against itself; a new corner-stone should be built into the edifice of our national, continental liberty, and those who "guard and support the structure," should accept, in all its comprehensiveness, the sentiment that all men are created equal, and that governments are established among men to defend and protect their inalienable rights to life, liberty, and the pursuit of happiness.

James T. Rapier

(1837–1883)

THE CIVIL RIGHTS BILL
February 4, 1875

Born the son of a wealthy planter in Florence, Alabama, in 1839, James T. Rapier was well educated by private tutors in his youth, and later at Montreal College in Canada, and at the University of Glasgow in Scotland. Rapier was elected to the U.S. Congress as the representative of the Second Congressional District of Alabama in 1872, whereupon he served one term before being defeated in his reelection bid. The following speech was delivered to Congress in support of the Civil Rights Act of 1875.

MR. SPEAKER, I had hoped there would be no protracted discussion on the civil-rights bill. It has been debated all over the country for the last seven years; twice it has done duty in our national political campaigns; and in every minor election during that time it has been pressed into service for the purpose of intimidating the weak white men who are inclined to support the republican ticket. I was certain until now that most persons were acquainted with its provisions, that they understood its meaning; therefore it was no longer to them the monster it had been depicted, that was to break down all social barriers, and compel one man to recognize another socially, whether agreeable to him or not.

I MUST CONFESS it is somewhat embarrassing for a colored man to urge the passage of this bill, because if he exhibits an earnestness in the matter and expresses a desire for its immediate passage, straightway he is charged with a desire for social equality, as explained by the demagogue and understood by the ignorant white man. But then it is just as embarrassing for him not to do so, for, if he remains silent while the struggle is being carried on around, and for him, he is liable to be charged with a want of interest in a matter that concerns him more than any one else, which is enough to make his friends desert his cause. So in steering away from Scylla I may run upon Charybdis. But the anomalous and, I may add, the supremely ridiculous position of the Negro at this time, in this country, compels me to say something. Here his condition is without comparison, parallel alone to itself. Just that the law recognizes my right upon this floor as a lawmaker, but that there is no law to secure to me any accommodations whatever while traveling here to discharge my duties as a Representative of a large and wealthy constituency. Here I am the peer of the proudest, but on a steamboat or car I am not equal to the most degraded. Is not this most anomalous and ridiculous?

What little I shall say will be more in the way of stating the case than otherwise, for I am certain I can add nothing to the arguments already made in behalf of the bill. If in the course of my remarks I should use language that may be considered inelegant, I have only to say that it shall be as elegant as that used by the opposition in discussing this measure; if undignified, it shall not be more so than my subject; if ridiculous, I enter the plea that the example has been set by the democratic side of the House, which claims the right to set examples.

I wish to say in justice to myself that no one regrets more than I do the necessity that compels one to the manor born to come in these halls with hat in hand (so to speak) to ask at the hands of his political peers the same public rights they enjoy. And I shall feel ashamed for my country if there be any foreigners present who have been lured to our shores by the popular but untruthful declaration that this land is the asylum of the oppressed, to hear a member of the highest legislative body in the world declare from his place, upon his responsibility as a Representative, that, notwithstanding his political position, he has no civil rights that another class is bound to respect.

Here a foreigner can learn what he cannot learn in any other country, that it is possible for a man to be half free and half slave, or, in other words, he will see that it is possible for a man to enjoy political rights while he is denied civil ones; here he will see a man legislating for a free people, while his own chains of slavery hang about him and are far more galling than any the foreigner left behind him; here he will see and what is not to be seen elsewhere, that position is no mantle of protection in our "land of the free and home of the brave"; for I am subjected to far more outrages and indignities in coming to and going from this capital in discharge of my public duties than any criminal in the country provided he be white. Instead of my position shielding me for insult, it too often invites it.

Let me cite a case. Not many months ago Mr. Cardozo, treasurer of the state of South Carolina, was on his way home from the West. His route lay through Atlanta. There he made request for a sleeping berth.

Not only was he refused this, but he was denied a seat in a first-class carriage, and the parties went so far as to threaten to take his life because he insisted upon his rights as a traveler. He was compelled, a most elegant and accomplished gentleman, to take a seat in the dirty smoking car, along with the traveling rabble, or else be left, to the detriment of his public duties.

I affirm, without the fear of contradiction, that any white ex-convict (I care not what may have been his crime, nor whether the hair on the shaven side of his head has had time to grow out or not) may start with me today to Montgomery, that all the way down he will be treated as a gentleman, while I will be treated as the convict. He will be allowed a berth in a sleeping car with all its comforts, while I will be forced into a dirty, rough box with the drunkards, apple sellers, railroad hands, and next to any dead that be in transit, regardless of how far decomposition may have progressed. Sentinels are placed at the doors of the better coaches, with positive instructions to keep persons of color out; and I must do them the justice to say that they guard these sacred portals with a vigilance that would have done credit to the flaming swords at the gates of Eden. Tender, pure, intelligent young ladies are forced to travel in this way if they are guilty of the crime of color, the only unpardonable sin known in our Christian and Bible lands, where sinning against the Holy Ghost (whatever that may be) sinks into significance when compared with the sin of color. If from any cause we are compelled to lay over, the best bed in the hotel is his if he can pay for it, while I am invariably turned away, hungry and cold, to stand around the railroad station until the departure of the next train, it matters not how long, thereby endangering my health, while my life and property are at the mercy of any highwayman who may wish to murder and rob me.

And I state without the fear of being gainsaid, the statement of the gentleman from Tennessee to the contrary notwithstanding, that there is not an inn between Washington and Montgomery, a distance of more than a thousand miles, that will accommodate me to bed or meal. Now, then, is there a man upon this floor who is so heartless, whose breast is so void of the better feelings, as to say that this brutal custom needs no regulation? I hold that it does and that Congress is the body to regulate it. Authority for its action is found not only in the Fourteenth Amendment to the Constitution, but by virtue of that amendment (which makes all persons born here citizens) authority is found in Article 4, Section 2, of the federal Constitution, which declares in positive language that "the citizens of each state shall have the same rights as the citizens of the several states." Let me read Mr. Brightly's comment upon this clause; he is considered good authority, I believe. In describing the several rights he says they may all be comprehended under the following general heads: "Protection by the government; the enjoyment of life and liberty, with the right to acquire and possess property of every kind, and to pursue and obtain happiness and safety; the right of a citizen of one state to pass through or to reside in any other state for purposes of trade, agriculture, professional pursuits, or otherwise."

It is very clear that the right of locomotion without hindrance and everything pertaining thereto is embraced in this clause; and every lawyer knows if any white man in antebellum times had been refused first-class passage in a steamboat or car, who was free from any contagious disease, and was compelled to go on deck of a boat or into a baggage car, and any accident had happened to him while he occupied that place, a lawsuit would have followed and damages would have been given by any jury to the plaintiff; and whether any accident had happened or not in the case I have referred to, a suit would have been brought for a denial of rights, and no one doubts what would have been the verdict. White men had rights then that common carriers were compelled to respect, and I demand the same for the colored men now.

Mr. Speaker, whether this deduction from the clause of the Constitution just read was applicable to the Negro prior to the adoption of the several late amendments to our organic law is now a question, but that it does apply to him in his new relations no intelligent man will dispute. Therefore I come to the national, instead of going to the local legislatures for relief, as has been suggested, because the grievance is national and not local; because Congress is the lawmaking power of the general government, whose duty it is to see that there be no unjust and odious discriminations made between citizens. I look to the government in the place of the several states, because it claims my first allegiance, exacts at my hands strict obedience to its laws, and because it promises in the implied contract between every citizen and the government to protect my life and property. I have fulfilled my part of the contract to the extent I have been called upon, and I demand that the government, through Congress, do likewise. Every day my life and property are exposed, are left to the mercy of others, and will be so as long as every hotelkeeper, railroad conductor and steamboat captain can refuse me with impunity the accommodations common to other travelers. I hold further, if the government cannot secure the citizen his guaranteed rights it ought not to call upon him to perform the same duties that are performed by another class of citizen who are in the free enjoyment of every civil and political right.

Sir, I submit that I am degraded as long as I am denied the public privileges common to other men, and that the members of this House are correspondingly degraded by recognizing my political equality while I occupy such humiliating position. What a singular attitude for lawmakers of this great nation to assume, rather come down to me than allow me to go up to them. Sir, did you ever reflect that this is the only Christian country where poor, finite man is held responsible for the crimes of the infinite God whom you profess to worship? But it is; I am held to answer for the crime of color, when I was not consulted in the matter. Had I been consulted, and my future fully described, I think I should have objected to being born in this Gospel land. The excuse offered for all this inhuman treatment is that they consider the Negro inferior to the white man, intellectually and morally. This reason might have been offered and probably accepted as truth some years ago, but not one now believes him incapable of a high order of culture, except someone who is himself below the average of mankind in natural endowments. This is not the reason, as I shall show before I have done.

Sir, there is a cowardly propensity in the human heart that delights in oppressing somebody else, and in the gratification of this base desire we always select a victim that can be outraged with safety. As a general thing, the Jew has been the subject in most parts of the world; but here the Negro is the most available for this purpose; for this reason in part he was seized upon, and not because he is naturally inferior to anyone else. Instead of his enemies believing him to be incapable of a high order of mental culture, they have shown that they believe the reverse to be true, by taking the most elaborate pains to prevent his development. And the smaller the caliber of the white man the more frantically has he fought to prevent the intellectual and moral progress of the Negro, for a simple but good reason that he has most to fear from such a result. He does not wish to see the Negro approach the high moral standard of a man and gentleman.

Let me call your attention to a case in point. Some time since, a well-dressed colored man was traveling from Augusta to Montgomery. The train on which he was stopped at a dinner house. The crowd around the depot, seeing him well dressed, fine-looking, and polite, concluded he must be a gentleman (which was more than their righteous souls could stand), and straightway they commenced to abuse him. And, sir, he had to go into the baggage car, open his trunks, show his cards, faro bank, dice, et cetera, before they would give him any peace; or, in other words, he was forced to give satisfactory evidence that he was not a man who was working to elevate the moral and intellectual standards of the Negro before they would respect him. I have always found more prejudice existing in the breast of men who have feeble minds and are conscious of it, than in the breast of those who have towering intellects and are aware of it. Henry Ward Beecher reflected the feelings of the latter class when on a certain occasion he said: "Turn the Negro loose; I am not afraid to run the race of life with him." He could afford to say this, all white men cannot; but what does the other class say? "Build a Chinese wall between the Negro and the school house, discourage in him pride of character and honest ambition, cut him off from every avenue that leads to the higher grounds of intelligence and usefulness, and then challenge him to a contest upon the highway of life to decide the question of superiority of race." By their acts, not by their words, the civilized world can and will judge how honest my opponents are in their declarations that I am naturally inferior to them. No one is surprised that this class opposes the passage of the civil-rights bill, for if the Negro were allowed the same opportunities, the same rights of locomotion, the same rights to comfort in travel, how could they prove themselves better than the Negro?

Mr. Speaker, it was said, I believe by the gentleman from Kentucky, [MR. BECK,] that the people of the South, particularly his state, were willing to accord the colored man all the rights they believe him guaranteed by the Constitution. No one doubts this assertion. But the difficulty is they do not acknowledge that I am entitled to any rights under the organic law. I am forced to this conclusion by reading the platforms of the democratic party in the several states. Which one declares that that party believes in the constitutionality of the Reconstruction Acts or the several amendments? But upon the other hand, they question the constitutionality of every measure that is advanced to ameliorate the condition of the colored man; and so skeptical have the Democracy become respecting the Constitution, brought about by their unsuccessful efforts to find constitutional objections to every step that is taken to elevate the Negro, that now they begin to doubt the constitutionality of the Constitution itself. The most they have agreed to do, is to obey present laws bearing on manhood suffrage until they are repealed by Congress or decided to be unconstitutional by the Supreme Court.

Let me read what the platform of the democratic party in Alabama has to say on this point:

The democratic and conservative party of the State of Alabama, in entering upon the contest for the redemption of the state government from the radical usurpers who now control it, adopt and declare as their platform—

1. That we stand ready to obey the Constitution of the United States and the laws passed in pursuance thereof; and the constitution and law of the State of Alabama, so long as they remain in force and unrepealed.

I will, however, take the gentleman at his word; but must be allowed to ask if so why was it, even after the several amendments had been officially announced to be part of the Federal Constitution, that his State and others refused to allow the Negro to testify in their courts against a white man? If they believed he should be educated (and surely this is a right) why was it that his school houses were burned down, and the teachers who had gone down on errands of mercy to carry light into dark places driven off, and in some places killed? If they believe the Negro should vote, (another right, as I understand the Constitution,) why was it that Ku Klux Klans were organized to prevent him from exercising the right of an American citizen, namely, casting the ballot—the very thing they said he had a right to do?

The professed belief and practice are sadly at variance, and must be intelligently harmonized before I can be made to believe that they are willing to acknowledge that I have any rights under the Constitution or elsewhere. He boasts of the magnanimity of Kentucky in allowing the Negro to vote without qualification, while to enjoy the same privilege in Massachusetts he is required to read the constitution of that State. He was very unhappy in this comparison. Why, sir, his State does not allow the Negro to vote at all. When was the constitution of Kentucky amended so as to grant him the elective franchise? They vote there by virtue of the fifteenth amendment alone, independent of the laws and constitution of that Commonwealth; and they would to-day disfranchise him if it could be done without affecting her white population. The Old Bay State waited for no "act of Congress" to force her to justice to all of her citizens, but in *ante bellum* days provided in her constitution that all male persons who could read and write should be entitled to suffrage. That was a case of equality before the law, and who had a right to complain? There is nothing now in the amended Federal Constitution to prevent Kentucky from adopting the same kind of clause in her constitution, when the convention meets to revise the organic law of that State, I venture the assertion that you will never hear a word about it; but it will not be out of any regard for her colored citizens, but the respect for that army of fifty-thousand ignorant white men she has within her borders, many of whom I see very time I pass through that State, standing around the several depots continually harping on the stereotyped phrase, "The damned Negro won't work."

I would not be surprised though if she should do better in the future. I remember when a foreigner was just as unpopular in Kentucky as the Negro is now; when the majority of the people of that State were opposed to according the foreigner the same rights they claimed for themselves; when that class of people were mobbed in the streets of her principal cities on account of their political faith, just as they have done the Negro of the last seven years. But what do you see to-day? One of that then proscribed class is Kentucky's chief Representative upon this floor. Is not this an evidence of a returning sense of justice? If so, would it not be reasonable to predict that she will in the near future send one of her now proscribed class to aid him in representing her interests upon this floor?

Mr. Speaker, there is another member of this body who has opposed the passage of this bill very earnestly, whose position in the country and peculiar relations to the Government compel me to refer to him before I conclude. I allude to the gentleman from Georgia, [MR. STEPHENS]. He returns to this House after an absence of many years with the same old ideas respecting State-rights that he carried away with him. He has not advanced a step; but unfortunately for him the American people have, and no longer consider him a fit expounder of our organic law. Following to its legitimate conclusion the doctrine of State-rights, (which of itself is secession), he deserted the flag of his country, followed his State out of the Union, and a long and bloody war followed. With its results most men are acquainted and recognize; but he, Bourbon-like, comes back saying the very same things he used to say and swearing by the same gods he swore by in other days. He seems not to know that the ideas which he so ably advanced for so many years were by the war swept away, along with that system of slavery which he intended should be the chief corner-stone, precious and elect, of the transitory kingdom over which he was second ruler.

Sir, the most of us have seen the play of Rip Van Winkle, who was said to have slept twenty years in the Katskill Mountains. On his return he found that the small trees had grown up to be large ones; the village of Falling Waters had improved beyond his recollection; the little children that used to play around his knees and ride into the village upon his back had grown up to be men and women and assumed the responsibilities of life; most of his friends, including Nick Vedder, had gone to that bourn whence no traveler returns; but, saddest of all, his child, "Mene," could not remember him. No one can see him in his efforts to recall the scenes of other days without being moved almost to tears. This, however, is fiction. The life and actions of the gentleman from Georgia most happily illustrate this character. This is a case where truth is stranger than fiction; and when he comes into these Halls advocating the same old ideas after an absence of so many years, during which time we have had a conflict of arms such as the world never saw, that revolutionized the entire body-politic, he stamps himself as a living "Rip Van Winkle."

I reiterate, that the principles of "State-rights," for the recognition of which, he now contends, are the ones that were in controversy during our late civil strife. The arguments *pro* and *con* were heard in the roar of battle, amid the shrieks of the wounded, and the groans of the dying; and the decision was rendered amid shouts of victory by the Union soldiers.

With it all appear to be familiar except him, and for his information I will state that upon this question an appeal was taken from the forum to the sword, the highest tribunal known to man, that it was then and there decided that National rights are paramount to State-rights, and that liberty and equality before the law should be coextensive with the jurisdiction of the Stars and Stripes. And I will further inform him that the bill now pending is simply to give practical effect to that decision.

I sympathize with him in his inability to understand this great change. When he left here the Negro was a chattel, exposed for sale in the market places within a stone's throw of the Capitol; so near that the shadow of the Goddess of Liberty reflected by rising sun would fall within the slave-pen as a forcible reminder that there was no hopeful day, nothing bright in the future, for the poor slave. Then no Negro was allowed to enter these Halls and hear discussions on subjects that most interested him. The words of lofty cheer that fell from the lips of Wade, Giddings, Julian, and others were not allowed to fall upon his ear. Then, not more than three Negroes were allowed to assemble at any place in the capital of the nation without special permission from the city authorities. But on his return he finds that the slave-pens have been torn down, and upon their ruins temples of learning have been erected; he finds that the Goddess of Liberty is no longer compelled to cover her radiant face while she weeps for our national shame, but looks with pride and satisfaction upon a free and regenerated land; he finds that the laws and regulations respecting the assembling of Negroes are no longer in force, but on the contrary he can see on any public holiday the Butler Zouaves, a fine-looking company of colored men, on parade.

Imagine, if you can, what would have been the effect of such a sight in this city twelve years ago. Then one Negro soldier would have caused utter consternation. Congress would have adjourned; the Cabinet would have sought protection elsewhere; the President would have declared martial law; troops and marines would have been ordered out; and I cannot tell all that would have happened; but now such a sight does not excite a ripple on the current of affairs; but over all, and worse to him than all, he finds the Negro here, not only a listener but a participant in debate. While I sympathize with him in his inability to comprehend his marvelous change, I must say in all earnestness that one who cannot understand and adjust himself to the new order of things is poorly qualified to teach this nation the meaning of our amended Constitution. The tenacity with which he sticks to his purpose through all the vicissitudes of life is commendable, though his views be objectionable.

While the chief of the late confederacy is away in Europe fleeing the wrath to come in the shape of Joe Johnston's history of the war, his lieutenant, with a boldness that must challenge the admiration of the most impudent, comes into these Halls and seeks to commit the nation through Congress to the doctrine of State-rights, and thus save it from the general work that followed the collapse of the rebellion. He had no other business here. Read his speech on the pending bill; his argument was cunning, far more ingenious than ingenuous. He does not deny the need or justness of the measure, but claims that the several States have exclusive jurisdiction of the same. I am not so willing as some others to believe in the sincerity of his assertions concerning the rights of the colored man. If he were honest in this matter, why is it he never recommended such a measure to the Georgia Legislature? If the several States had secured to all classes within their borders the rights contemplated in this bill, we would have had no need to come here; but they having failed to do their duty, after having had ample opportunity, the General Government is called upon to exercise its right in the matter.

Mr. Speaker, time will not allow me to review the history of the American Negro, but I must pause here long enough to say that he has not been properly treated by this nation; he has purchased and paid for all, and for more than, he has yet received. Whatever liberty he enjoys has been paid for over and over again by more than two hundred years of forced toil; and for such citizenship as is allowed him he paid the full measure of his blood, the dearest price required at the hands of any citizen. In every contest, from the beginning of the Revolutionary struggle down to the War Between the States, has he been prominent. But we all remember in our late war when the government was so hard pressed for troops to sustain the cause of the Union, when it was so difficult to fill up the ranks that had been so fearfully decimated by disease and the bullet; when every train that carried to the front a number of fresh soldiers brought back a corresponding number of wounded and sick ones; when grave doubts as to the success of the Union arms had seized upon the minds of some of the most sanguine friends of the government; when strong men took counsel of their fears; when those who had all their lives received the fostering care of the nation were hesitating as to their duty in that trying hour, and others questioning if it were not better to allow the star of this Republic to go down and thus be blotted out from the great map of nations than to continue the bloodshed; when gloom and despair were widespread; when the last rays of hope had nearly sunk below our political horizon, how the Negro then came forward and offered himself as a sacrifice in the place of the nation, made bare his breast to the steel, and in it received the thrusts of the bayonet that were aimed at the life of the nation by the soldiers of that government in which the gentleman from Georgia figured as second officer.

Sir, the valor of the colored soldier was tested on many a battlefield, and today his bones lie bleaching beside every hill and in every valley from the Potomac to the Gulf; whose mute eloquence in behalf of equal rights for all before the law, is and ought to be far more persuasive than any poor language I can command.

Mr. Speaker, nothing short of a complete acknowledgment of my manhood will satisfy me. I have no compromises to make, and shall unwillingly accept any. If I were to say that I would be content with less than any other member upon this floor I would forfeit whatever respect any one here might entertain for me, and would thereby furnish the best possible evidence that I do not and cannot appreciate the rights of a free-man—just what I am charged with by my political enemies. I cannot willingly accept anything less than my full measure of rights as a man, because I am unwilling to present myself as a candidate for the brand of inferiority, which will be as plain and lasting as the mark of Cain. If I am to be thus branded, the country must do it against my solemn protest.

Sir, in order that I might know something of the feelings of a freeman, a privilege denied me in the land of my birth, I left home last year and traveled six months in foreign lands, and the moment I put my foot upon the deck of a ship that unfurled a foreign flag from its masthead, distinctions on account of my color ceased. I am not aware that my presence on board the steamer put her off her course. I believe we made the trip in the usual time. It was in other countries than my own that I was not a stranger, that I could approach a hotel without the fear that the door would be slammed in my face. Sir, I feel this humiliation very keenly; it dwarfs my manhood, and certainly it impairs my usefulness as a citizen.

The other day when the centennial bill was under discussion I would have been glad to say a word in its favor, but how could I? How would I appear at the centennial celebration of our national freedom, with my own galling chains of slavery hanging about me? I could no more rejoice on that occasion in my present condition than the Jews could sing in their wonted style as they sat as captives beside the Babylonish streams; but I look forward to the day when I shall be in the full enjoyment of the rights of a freeman, with the same hope they indulged, that they would again return to their native land. I can no more forget my manhood, than they could forget Jerusalem.

After all, this question resolves itself to this: either I am a man or I am not a man. If one, I am entitled to all the rights, privileges and immunities common to any other class in this country; if not a man, I have no right to vote, no right to a seat here; if no right to vote, then 20 percent of the members on this floor have no right here, but, on the contrary, hold their seats in violation of the law. If the Negro has no right to vote, then one eighth of your Senate consists of members who have no shadow of a claim to the places they occupy; and if no right to vote, a half-dozen governors in the South figure as usurpers.

This is the legitimate conclusion of the arguments, that the Negro is not a man and is not entitled to all the public rights common to other men, and you cannot escape it. But when I press my claims I am asked, "Is it good policy?" My answer is, "Policy is out of the question; it has nothing to do with it; that you can have no policy in dealing with your citizens; that there must be one law for all; that in this case justice is the only standard to be used, and you can no more divide justice than you can divide Deity." On the other hand, I am told that I must respect the prejudices of others. Now, sir, no one respects reasonable and intelligent prejudice more than I. I respect religious prejudices, for example, these I can comprehend. But how can I have respect for the prejudices that prompt a man to turn up his nose at the males of a certain race, while at the same time he has a fondness for the females of the same race to the extent of cohabitation? Out of four poor unfortunate colored women, who from poverty were forced to go to the lying-in branch of the Freedman's Hospital here in the District last year, three gave birth to children whose fathers were white men, and I venture to say that if they were members of this body, would vote against the civil-rights bill. Do you, can you wonder at my want of respect for this kind of prejudice? To make me feel uncomfortable appears to be the highest ambition of many white men. It is to them a positive luxury, which they seem to indulge at every opportunity.

I have never sought to compel any one, white or black, to associate with me, and never shall; nor do I wish to be compelled to associate with any one. If a man does not wish to ride with me in the streetcar, I shall not object to his hiring a private conveyance; if he does not wish to ride with me from here to Baltimore, who shall complain if he charter a special train? For a man to carry out his prejudices in this way would be manly and would leave no cause for complaint, but to crowd me out of the usual conveyance into an uncomfortable place with persons for whose manners I have a dislike, whose language is not fit for ears polite, is decidedly unmanly and cannot be submitted to tamely by anyone who has a particle of self-respect.

Sir, this whole thing grows out of a desire to establish a system of "caste," an anti-republican principle, in our free country. In Europe they have princes, dukes, lords, &c., in contradistinction to the middle classes and peasants. Further East they have the brahmans or priests, who rank above the sudras or laborers. In those countries distinctions are based upon blood and position. Every one there understands the custom and no one complains. They, poor innocent creatures, pity our condition, look down upon us with a kind of royal compassion, because they think we have no tangible lines of distinction, and therefore speak of our society as being vulgar. But let not our friends beyond the seas lay the flattering unction to their souls that we are without distinctive lines; that we have no nobility; for we are blessed with both. Our distinction is color, (which would necessarily exclude the brahmans,) and our lines are much broader than anything they know of. Here a drunken white man is not only equal to a drunken Negro, (as would be the case anywhere else,) but superior to the most sober and orderly one; here an ignorant white man is not only the equal of an unlettered Negro, but is superior to the most cultivated; here our nobility cohabit with our female peasants, and they throw up their hands in holy horror when a male of the same class enters a restaurant to get a meal, and if he insist upon being accommodated our scion of royalty will leave and go to the arms of his colored mistress and there pour out his soul's complaint, tell her of the impudence of the "damned nigger" in coming to a table where a white man was sitting.

What poor, simple-minded creatures these foreigners are. They labor under the decision that they monopolize the knowledge of the courtesies due from one gentleman to another. How I rejoice to know that it is a delusion. Sir, I wish some of them could have been present to hear the representative of the F.F.V.'s upon this floor (and I am told that that is the highest degree that society has yet reached in this country) address one of his peers, who dared asked him a question, in this style; "I am talking to white men." Suppose Mr. Gladstone—who knows no man but by merit—who in violation of our custom entertained the colored jubilee singers at his home last summer, or the Duke of Broglie, had been present and heard this eloquent remark drop from the lips of this classical and knightly member, would they not have hung their heads in shame at their ignorance of politeness, and would they not have returned home, repaired to their libraries, and betaken themselves to the study of Chesterfield on manners? With all these absurdities staring them in the face, who can wonder that foreigners laugh at our ideas of distinction?

Mr. Speaker, though there is not a line in this bill the Democracy approve of, yet they made the most noise about the school clause. Dispatches are freely sent over the wires as to what will be done with the common-school system in the several Southern states in the event this bill becomes a law. I am not surprised at this, but, on the other hand, I looked for it. Now what is the force of that school clause? It simply provides that all the children in every state where there is a school system supported in whole or in part by general taxation shall have equal advantages of school privileges. So that if perfect and ample accommodations are not made convenient for all the children, then any child has the right to go to any school where they do exist. And that is all there is in this school clause. I want some one to tell me of any measure that was intended to benefit the Negro that they have approved of. Of which one did they fail to predict evil? They declared if the Negroes were emancipated that the country would be laid waste, and that in the end he would starve, because he could not take care of himself. But this was a mistake. When the Reconstruction acts were passed and the colored men in my state were called upon to express through the ballot whether Alabama should return to the Union or not, white men threw up their hands in holy horror and declared if the Negro voted that never again would they deposit another ballot. But how does the matter stand now? Some of those very men are in the Republican ranks, and I have known them to grow hoarse in shouting for our platforms and candidates. They hurrah for our principles with all the enthusiasm of a newborn soul, and, sir, so zealous have they become that in looking at them I am amazed and am often led to doubt my faith and feel ashamed for my lukewarmness. And those who have not joined our party are doing their utmost to have the Negro vote with them. I have met them in the cabins night and day where they were imploring him, for the sake of old times, to come up and vote with them.

I submit, Mr. Speaker, that political prejudices prompt the Democracy to oppose this bill as much as anything else. In the campaign of 1868 Joe Williams, an uncouth and rather notorious colored man, was employed as a general Democratic canvasser in the South. He was invited to Montgomery to enlighten us, and while there he stopped at one of the best hotels in the city, one that would not dare entertain me. He was introduced at the meeting by the chairman of the Democratic executive committee as a learned and elegant, as well as eloquent, gentleman. In North Alabama he was invited to speak at the Seymour and Blair barbecue, and did address one of the largest audiences, composed largely of ladies, that ever assembled in that part of the state. This I can prove by my simon-pure Democratic colleague, Mr. Sloss, for he was chairman of the committee of arrangements on that occasion, and I never saw so radiant with good humor in all my life as when he had the honor of introducing "his friend," Mr. Williams. In that case they were extending their courtesies to a coarse, vulgar stranger, because he was a Democrat, while at the same time they were hunting me down as a partridge on the mount, night and day, with their Ku Klux Klan, simply because I was a Republican and refused to bow at the foot of their Baal. I might enumerate many instances of this kind, but I forbear. But to come down to a later period, the Greeley campaign. The colored men who were employed to canvass North Carolina in the interest of the Democratic party were received at all the hotels as other men and treated, I am informed, with marked distinction. And in the state of Louisiana a very prominent colored gentleman saw proper to espouse the Greeley cause, and when the fight was over and the McEnery government saw fit to send on a committee to Washington to present their case to the

President, this colored gentleman was selected as one of that committee. On arriving in the city of New Orleans prior to his departure he was taken to the St. Charles, the most aristocratic hotel in the South. When they started he occupied a berth in the sleeping car; at every eating house he was treated like the rest of them, no distinction whatever. And when they arrived in Montgomery, I was at the depot, just starting for New York. Not only did the conductor refuse to allow me a berth in the sleeping car, but I was also denied a seat in the first-class carriage. Now, what was the difference between us? Nothing but our political faith. To prove this I have only to say that just a few months before this happened, he, along with Frederick Douglass and others, was denied the same privileges he enjoyed in coming here. And now that he has returned to the right party again I can tell him that never more will he ride in another sleeping car in the South unless this bill becomes law. There never was a truer saying than that circumstances alter cases.

Mr. Speaker, to call this land the asylum of the oppressed is a misnomer, for upon all sides I am treated as a pariah. I hold that the solution of this whole matter is to enact such laws and prescribe such penalties for their violation as will prevent any person from discriminating against another in public places on account of color. No one asks, no one seeks the passage of law that will interfere with any one's private affairs. But I do ask the enactment of a law to secure me in the enjoyment of public privileges. But when I ask this I am told that I must wait for public opinion; that it is a matter that cannot be forced by law. While I admit that public opinion is a power, and in many cases is a law of itself, yet I cannot lose sight of the fact that both statute law and the law of necessity manufacture public opinion. I remember it was unpopular to enlist Negro soldiers in our late war, and after they enlisted it was equally unpopular to have them fight in the same battles; but when it became a necessity in both cases, public opinion soon came around to that point. No white father objected to the Negro's becoming food for powder if thereby his son could be saved. No white woman objected to the Negro marching in the same ranks and fighting in the same battles if by that her husband could escape burial in our savannas and return to her and her little ones.

Suppose there had been no Reconstruction Acts nor amendments to the Constitution, when would public opinion in the South have suggested the propriety of giving me the ballot? Unaided by law when would public opinion have prompted the administration to appoint members of my race to represent this government at foreign courts? It is said by some well-meaning men that the colored man has now every right under the common law; in reply I wish to say that that kind of law commands very little respect when applied to the rights of colored men in my portion of the country; the only law that we have any regard for is uncommon law of the most positive character. And I repeat, if you will place upon your statute books laws that will protect me in my rights, that public opinion will speedily follow.

Mr. Speaker, I trust this bill will become law, because it is a necessity, and because it will put an end to all legislation on this subject. It does not and cannot contemplate any such ideas as social equality; nor is there any man upon this floor so silly as to believe that there can be any law enacted or enforced that would compel one man to recognize another as his equal socially; if there be, he ought not be here, and I have only to say that they have sent him to the wrong public building. I would oppose such a bill as earnestly as the gentleman from North Carolina, whose associations and cultivations have been of such a nature as to lead him to select the crow as his standard of grandeur and excellence in the place of the eagle, the hero of all birds and our national emblem of pride and power. I will tell him that I have seen many of his race to whose level I should object to being dragged.

Sir, it matters not how much men may differ upon the question of state and national rights; here is one class of rights, however, that we all agree upon, namely, individual rights, which include the right of every man to select associates for himself and family, and to say who shall and who shall not visit at his house. This right is God-given and custom-sanctioned, and there is, and there can be, no power overruling your decision in this matter. Let this bill become law, and not only will it do much toward giving rest to this weary country on this subject, completing the manhood of my race and perfecting his citizenship, but it will take him from the political arena as a topic of discussion where he has done duty for the last fifty years, and thus freed from anxiety respecting his political standing, hundreds of us will abandon the political fields who are there from necessity, and not from choice, and seek other and more pleasant ones; and thus relieved, it will be the aim of the colored man as well as his duty and interest, to become a good citizen, and to do all in his power to advance the interests of a common country.

Alexander Crummell

(1819–1898)

THE BLACK WOMAN OF THE SOUTH:
HER NEGLECTS AND HER NEEDS
August 15, 1883

Alexander Crummell was born in New York City, the son of an African prince and a free mother. He attended an interracial school in Canaan, New Hampshire, and was ordained as an Episcopalian minister in the Diocese of Massachusetts in 1844. After spending twenty years as a missionary in Liberia, Crummell returned to the United States. He founded St. Luke's Episcopal Church in Washington, D.C.; led the Conference of Church Workers Among Colored People in 1883; and founded the American Negro Academy in 1897. Crummell gave the following speech to the Freeman's Aid Society at the Methodist Episcopal Church in Ocean Grove, New Jersey.

It is an age clamorous everywhere for the dignities, the grand prerogatives, and the glory of woman. There is not a country in Europe where she has not risen somewhat above the degradation of centuries, and pleaded successfully for a new position and a higher vocation. As the result of this new reformation we see her, in our day, seated in the lecture-rooms of ancient universities, rivaling her brothers in the fields of literature, the grand creators of ethereal art, the participants in noble civil franchises, the moving spirit in grand reformations, and the guide, agent, or assistant in all the noblest movements for the civilization and regeneration of man.

In these several lines of progress the American woman has run on in advance of her sisters in every other quarter of the globe. The advantage, she has received, the rights and prerogatives she has secured for herself, are unequaled by any other class of women in the world. It will not be thought amiss, then, that I come here to-day to present to your consideration the one grand exception to this general superiority of women, viz., *The black woman of the South.*

* * * * *

The rural or plantation population of the South was made up almost entirely of people of pure Negro blood. And this brings out also the other disastrous fact, namely, that this large black population has been living from the time of their introduction into America, a period of more than two hundred years, in a state of unlettered rudeness. The Negro all this time has been an intellectual starveling. This has been more especially the condition of the black woman of the South. Now and then a black man has risen above the debased condition of his people. Various causes would contribute to the advantage of the *men:* the relation of servants to superior masters; attendance at courts with them; their presence at political meetings; listening to table-talk behind their chairs; traveling as valets; the privilege of books and reading in great houses, and with indulgent masters—all these served to lift up a black *man* here and there to something like superiority. But no such fortune fell to the lot of the plantation woman. The black woman of the South was left perpetually in a state of hereditary darkness and rudeness.

* * * * *

In her girlhood all the delicate tenderness of her sex was rudely outraged. In the field, in the rude cabin, in the press-room, in the factory, she was thrown into the companionship of coarse and ignorant men. No chance was given her for delicate reserve or tender modesty. From her girlhood she was the doomed victim of the grossest passions. All the virtues of her sex were utterly ignored. If the instinct of chastity asserted itself, then she had to fight like a tigress for the ownership and possession of her own person; and, ofttimes, had to suffer pains and lacerations for her virtuous self-assertion. When she reached maturity all the tender instincts of her womanhood were ruthlessly violated. At the age of marriage—always prematurely anticipated under slavery—she was mated, as the stock of the plantation were mated, *not* to be the companion of a loved and chosen husband, but to be the breeder of human cattle, for the field or the auction-block. With that mate she went out, morning after morning to toil, as a common field-hand. As it was *his,* so likewise was it her lot to wield the heavy hoe, or to follow the plow, or to gather in the crops. She was a "hewer of wood and a drawer of water." She was a common field-hand. She had to keep her place in the gang from morn till eve, under the burden of a heavy task, or under the stimulus or the fear of a cruel lash. She was a picker of cotton. She labored at the sugar-mill and in the tobacco-factory. When, through weariness or sickness, she had fallen behind her allotted task, there came, as punishment, the fearful stripes upon her shrinking, lacerated flesh.

Her home life was of the most degrading nature. She lived in the rudest huts, and partook of the coarsest food, and dressed in the scantiest garb, and slept, in multitudinous cabins, upon the hardest boards.

Thus she continued a beast of burden down to the period of those maternal anxieties, which, in ordinary civilized life, give repose, quiet, and care to expectant mothers. But, under the slave system, few such relaxations were allowed. And so it came to pass that little children were ushered into this world under conditions which many cattle-raisers would not suffer for their flocks or herds. Thus she became the mother of children. But even then there was for her no suretyship of motherhood, or training, or control. Her own offspring were *not* her own. She and husband and children were all the property of others. All these sacred ties were constantly snapped and cruelly sundered. *This* year she had one husband; and next year, through some auction sale, she might be separated from him and mated to another. There was no sanctity of family, no binding tie of marriage, none of the fine felicities and the endearing affections of home. None of these things was the lot of Southern black women. Instead thereof, a gross barbarism which tended to blunt the tender sensibilities, to obliterate feminine delicacy and womanly shame, came down as her heritage from generation to generation; and it seems a miracle of providence and grace that, notwithstanding these terrible circumstances, so much struggling virtue lingered amid these rude cabins, that so much womanly worth and sweetness abided in their bosoms, as slave-holders themselves have borne witness to.

But some of you will ask: "Why bring up these sad memories of the past? Why distress us with these dead and departed cruelties?" Alas, my friends, these are not dead things. Remember that

> "The evil that men do lives after them."

The evil of gross and monstrous abominations, the evil of great organic institutions crop out long after the departure of the institutions themselves. If you go to Europe you will find not only the roots, but likewise many of the deadly fruits of the old Feudal system still surviving in several of its old states and kingdoms. So, too, with slavery. The eighteen years of freedom have not obliterated all its deadly marks from either the souls or bodies of the black woman. The conditions of life, indeed, have been modified since emancipation; but it still maintains that the black woman is the Pariah woman of this land! We have, indeed, degraded women, immigrants, from foreign lands. In their own countries some of them were so low in the social scale that they were yoked with the cattle to plow the fields. They were rude, unlettered, coarse, and benighted. But when they reach *this* land there comes an end to their degraded condition.

> "They touch our country and their shackles fall."

As soon as they become grafted into the stock of American life they partake at once of all its large gifts and its noble resources.

Not so with the black woman of the South. Freed, legally she has been; but the act of emancipation had no talismanic influence to reach to and alter and transform her degrading social life.

When that proclamation was issued she might have heard the whispered words in her every hut, "Open, Sesame"; but, so far as her humble domicile and her degraded person were concerned, there was no invisible but gracious Genii who, on the instant, could transmute the rudeness of her hut into instant elegance, and change the crude surroundings of her home into neatness, taste, and beauty.

The truth is, "Emancipation Day" found her a prostrate and degraded being; and, although it has brought numerous advantages to her sons, it has produced but the simplest changes in her social and domestic condition. She is still the crude, rude, ignorant mother. Remote from cities, the dweller still in the old plantation hut, neighboring to the sulky, disaffected master class, who still think her freedom was a personal robbery of themselves, none of the "fair humanities" have visited her humble home. The light of knowledge has not fallen upon her eyes. The fine domesticities which give the charm to family life, and which, by the refinement and delicacy of womanhood, preserve the civilization of nations, have not come to *her*. She has still the rude, coarse labor of men. With her rude husband she still shares the hard service of a field-hand. Her house, which shelters, perhaps, some six or eight children, embraces but two rooms. Her furniture is of the rudest kind. The clothing of the household is scant and of the coarsest material, has ofttimes the garniture of rags; and for herself and offspring is marked, not seldom, by the absence of both hats and shoes. She has rarely been taught to sew, and the field labor of slavery times has kept her ignorant of the habitudes of neatness, and the requirements of order. Indeed, coarse food, coarse clothes, coarse living, coarse manners, coarse companions, coarse surroundings, coarse neighbors, both black and white, yea, every thing coarse, down to the coarse, ignorant, senseless religion, which excites her sensibilities and starts her passions, go to make up the life of the masses of black women in the hamlets and villages of the rural South.

This is the state of black womanhood. Take the girlhood of this same region, and it presents the same aspect, save that in large districts the white man has not forgotten the olden times of slavery and with indeed the deepest sentimental abhorrence of "amalgamation," still thinks that the black girl is to be perpetually the victim of his lust! In the larger towns and in cities our girls in common schools and academies are receiving superior culture. Of the 15,000 colored school teachers in the South, more than half are colored young women, educated since emancipation. But even these girls, as well as their more ignorant sisters in rude huts, are followed and tempted and insulted by the ruffianly element of Southern society, who think that black *men* have no rights which white men should regard, and black *women* no virtue which white men should respect!

And now look at the *vastness* of this degradation. If I had been speaking of the population of a city, or a town, or even a village, the tale would be a sad and melancholy one. But I have brought before you the condition of millions of women. According to the census of 1880 there were, in the Southern States, 3,327,678 females of all ages of the African race. Of these there were 674,365 girls between twelve and twenty, 1,522,696 between twenty and eighty. "These figures," remarks an observing friend of mine, "are startling!" And when you think that the masses of these women live in the rural districts; that they grow up in rudeness and ignorance; that their former masters are using few means to break up their hereditary degradation, you can easily take in the pitiful condition of this population, and forecast the inevitable future to multitudes of females unless a mighty special effort is made for the improvement of the black womanhood of the South.

I know the practical nature of the American mind, I know how the question of values intrudes itself into even the domain of philanthropy; and, hence, I shall not be astonished if the query suggests itself, whether special interest in the black woman will bring any special advantage to the American nation.

Let me dwell for a few moments upon this phase of the subject. Possibly the view I am about suggesting has never before been presented to the American mind. But, Negro as I am, I shall make no apology for venturing the claim that the Negress is one of the most interesting of all the classes of women on the globe. I am speaking of her, not as a perverted and degraded creature, but in her natural state, with her native instincts and peculiarities.

Let me repeat just here the words of a wise, observing, tender-hearted philanthropist, whose name and worth and words have attained celebrity. It is fully forty years ago since the celebrated Dr. Channing said: "We are holding in bondage one of the best races of the human family. The Negro is among the mildest, gentlest of men. He is singularly susceptible of improvement from abroad. . . . His nature is affectionate, easily touched, and hence he is more open to religious improvement than the white man. . . . The African carries with him much more than *we* the genius of a meek, long-suffering, loving virtue."

I should feel ashamed to allow these words to fall from my lips if it were not necessary to the lustration of the character of my black sisters of the South. I do not stand here to-day to plead for the black *man*. He is a man; and if he is weak he must go to the wall. He is a man; he must fight his own way, and if he is strong in mind and body, he can take care of himself. But for the mothers, sisters, and daughters of my race I have a right to speak. And when I think of their sad condition down South; think, too, that since the day of emancipation hardly any one has lifted up a voice in their behalf, I feel it a duty and a privilege to set forth their praises and to extol their excellencies. For, humble and benighted as she is, the black woman of the South is one of the queens of womanhood. If there is any other woman on this earth who in native aboriginal qualities is her superior, I know not where she is to be found; for, I do say, that in tenderness of feeling, in genuine native modesty, in large disinterestedness, in sweetness of disposition and deep humility, in unselfish devotedness, and in warm, motherly assiduities, the Negro woman is unsurpassed by any other woman on this earth.

The testimony to this effect is almost universal—our enemies themselves being witnesses. You know how widely and how continuously, for generations, the Negro has been traduced, ridiculed, derided. Some of you may remember the journals and the hostile criticisms of Coleridge and Trollope and Burton, West Indian and African travelers. Very many of you may remember the philosophical disquisitions of the ethnological school of 1847, the contemptuous dissertations of Hunt and Gliddon. But it is worthy of notice in all these cases that the sneer, the contempt, the bitter gibe, have been invariably leveled against the black *man*—never against the black woman! On the contrary, *she* has almost everywhere been extolled and eulogized. The black man was called a stupid, thick-lipped, flat-nosed, long-heeled, empty-headed animal; the link between the baboon and the human being, only fit to be a slave! But everywhere, even in the domains of slavery, how tenderly has the Negress been spoken of! She has been the nurse of childhood. To her all the cares and heart-griefs of youth have been intrusted. Thousands and tens of thousands in the West Indies and in our Southern States have risen up and told the tale of her tenderness, of her gentleness, patience, and affection. No other woman in the world has ever had such tributes to a high moral nature, sweet, gentle love, and unchanged devotedness. And by the memory of my own mother and dearest sisters I can declare it to be true!

Hear the tribute of Michelet: "The Negress, of all others, is the most loving, the most generating; and this, not only because of her youthful blood, but we must also admit, for the richness of her heart. She is loving among the loving, good among the good. (Ask the travelers whom she has so often saved.) Goodness is creative; it is fruitfulness; it is the very benediction of a holy act. The fact that woman is so fruitful I attribute to her treasures of tenderness, to that ocean of goodness which permeates her heart. . . . Africa is a woman. Her races are feminine. . . . In many of the black tribes of Central Africa the women rule, and they are as intelligent as they are amiable and kind."

The reference in Michelet to the generosity of the African woman to travelers brings to mind the incident in Mungo Park's travels, where the African women fed, nourished, and saved him. The men had driven him away. They would not even allow him to feed with the cattle; and so, faint, weary, and despairing, he went to a remote hut and lay down on the earth to die. One woman, touched with compassion, came to him, brought him food and milk, and at once he revived. Then he tells us of the solace and the assiduities of these gentle creatures for his comfort. I give you his own words: "The rites of hospitality thus performed toward a stranger in distress, my worthy benefactress, pointing to the mat, and telling me that I might sleep there without apprehension, called to the female part of her family which had stood gazing on me all the while in fixed astonishment, to resume the task of spinning cotton, in which they continued to employ themselves a great part of the night. They lightened their labors by songs, one of which was composed extempore, for I was myself the subject of it. It was sung by one of the young women, the rest joining in a sort of chime. The air was sweet and plaintive, and the words, literally translated, were these: 'The winds roared and the rains fell; the poor white man, faint and weary, came and sat under our tree. He has no mother to bring him milk, no wife to grind his corn. Let us pity the white man, no mother has he,'" etc.

Perhaps I may be pardoned the intrusion, just here, of my own personal experience. During a residence of nigh twenty years in West Africa, I saw the beauty and felt the charm of the native female character. I saw the native woman in her *heathen* state, and was delighted to see, in numerous tribes, that extraordinary sweetness, gentleness, docility, modesty, and especially those maternal solicitudes which make every African boy both gallant and defender of his mother.

I saw her in her *civilized* state, in Sierra Leone; saw precisely the same characteristics, but heightened, dignified, refined, and sanctified by the training of the schools, the refinements of civilization, and the graces of Christian sentiment and feeling. Of all the memories of foreign travel there are none more delightful than those of the families and the female friends of Freetown.

A French traveler speaks with great admiration of the black ladies of Hayti. "In the towns," he says, "I met all the charms of civilized life. The graces of the ladies of Port-au-Prince will never be effaced from my recollections."

It was, without doubt, the instant discernment of these fine and tender qualities which prompted the touching Sonnet of Wordsworth, written in 1802, on the occasion of the cruel exile of Negroes from France by the French Government:

"Driven from the soil of France, a female came
    From Calais with us, brilliant in array,
    A Negro woman like a lady gay,
Yet downcast as a woman fearing blame;
    Meek, destitute, as seemed, of hope or aim
    She sat, from notice turning not away,
But on all proffered intercourse did lay
    A weight of languid speech—or at the same
Was silent, motionless in eyes and face.
    Meanwhile those eyes retained their tropic fire
Which burning independent of the mind,
    Joined with the luster of her rich attire
To mock the outcast—O ye heavens, be kind!
And feel, thou earth, for this afflicted race!"

But I must remember that I am to speak not only of the neglects of the black woman, but also of her needs. And the consideration of her needs suggests the remedy which should be used for the uplifting of this woman from a state of brutality and degradation.

* * * * *

Ladies and gentlemen, since the day of emancipation millions of dollars have been given by the generous Christian people of the North for the intellectual training of the black race in this land. Colleges and universities have been built in the South, and hundreds of youth have been gathered within their walls. The work of your own Church in this regard has been magnificent and unrivaled, and the results which have been attained have been grand and elevating to the entire Negro race in America. The complement to all this generous and ennobling effort is the elevation of the black woman. Up to this day and time your noble philanthropy has touched, for the most part, the male population of the South, given them superiority, and stimulated them to higher aspirations. But a true civilization can only then be attained when the life of woman is reached, her whole being permeated by noble ideas, her fine taste enriched by culture, her tendencies to the beautiful gratified and developed, her singular and delicate nature lifted up to its full capacity; and then, when all these qualities are fully matured, cultivated and sanctified, all their sacred influences shall circle around ten thousand firesides, and the cabins of the humblest freedmen shall become the homes of Christian refinement and of domestic elegance through the influence and the charm of the uplifted and cultivated black woman of the South!

Booker T. Washington

(1856–1915)

ATLANTA EXPOSITION ADDRESS
October 18, 1895

Born into slavery in Franklin County, Virginia, Booker T. Washington moved with his family to West Virginia after emancipation, where he remained until enrolling at the Hampton Normal and Agricultural Institute in eastern Virginia (1872). After graduating in 1875, Washington went on to teach at Hampton and elsewhere, serving as the first principal of the Tuskegee Normal and Industrial Institute. Booker T. Washington's career as a public figure and civil rights leader took off with the following speech, which he delivered at the Atlanta Cotton States and International Exposition in Atlanta, Georgia.

MR. PRESIDENT and Gentlemen of the Board of Directors and Citizens:

One-third of the population of the South is of the Negro race. No enterprise seeking the material, civil, or moral welfare of this section can disregard this element of our population and reach the highest success. I but convey to you, Mr. President and Directors, the sentiment of the masses of my race when I say that in no way have the value and manhood of the American Negro been more fittingly and generously recognized than by the managers of this magnificent Exposition at every stage of its progress. It is a recognition that will do more to cement the friendship of the two races than any occurrence since the dawn of our freedom.

Not only this, but the opportunity here afforded will awaken among us a new era of industrial progress. Ignorant and inexperienced, it is not strange that in the first years of our new life we began at the top instead of at the bottom; that a seat in Congress or the state legislature was more sought than real estate or industrial skill; that the political convention or stump speaking had more attraction than starting a dairy farm or stockyard.

A ship lost at sea for many days suddenly sighted a friendly vessel. From the mast of the unfortunate vessel was seen a signal, "Water, water; we die of thirst!" The answer from the friendly vessel at once came back, "Cast down your bucket where you are." A second time the signal, "Water, send us water!" went up from the distressed vessel, and was answered, "Cast down your bucket where you are." And a third and fourth signal for water was answered, "Cast down your bucket where you are." The captain of the distressed vessel, at last heeding the injunction, cast down his bucket, and it came up full of fresh, sparkling water from the mouth of the Amazon River.

To those of my race who depend on bettering their condition in a foreign land or who underestimate the importance of cultivating friendly relations with the Southern white man, who is their next-door neighbor, I would say: "Cast down your bucket where you are"—cast it down, making friends in every manly way of the people of all races by whom you are surrounded.

Cast it down in agriculture, mechanics, in commerce, in domestic service, and in the professions. And in this connection it is well to bear in mind that whatever other sins the South may be called to bear, when it comes to business, pure and simple, it is in the South that the Negro is given a man's chance in the commercial world, and in nothing is this Exposition more eloquent than in emphasizing this chance. Our greatest danger is that in the great leap from slavery to freedom we may overlook the fact that the masses of us are to live by the productions of our hands, and fail to keep in mind that we shall prosper in proportion as we learn to dignify and glorify common labor and put brains and skill into the common occupations of life, shall prosper in proportion as we learn to draw the line between the superficial and the substantial, the ornamental gewgaws of life and the useful. No race can prosper till it learns that there is as much dignity in tilling a field as in writing a poem. It is at the bottom of life we must begin, and not at the top. Nor should we permit our grievances to overshadow our opportunities.

"Cast down your bucket where you are!"

To those of the white race who look to the incoming of those of foreign birth and strange tongue and habits for the prosperity of the South, were I permitted I would repeat what I say to my own race, "Cast down your bucket where you are." Cast it down among the eight millions of Negroes whose habits you know, whose fidelity and love you have tested in days when to have proved treacherous meant the ruin of your firesides. Cast down your bucket among these people who have, without strikes and labor wars, tilled your fields, cleared your forests, builded your railroads and cities, and brought forth treasures from the bowels of the earth, and helped make possible this magnificent representation of the progress of the South.

Casting down your bucket among my people, helping and encouraging them as you are doing on these grounds, and to education of head, hand, and heart, you will find that they will buy your surplus land, make blossom the waste places in your fields, and run your factories.

While doing this, you can be sure in the future, as in the past, that you and your families will be surrounded by the most patient, faithful, law-abiding, and unresentful people that the world has seen. As we have proved our loyalty to you in the past, in nursing your children, watching by the sick-bed of your mothers and fathers, and often following them with tear-dimmed eyes to their graves, so in the future, in our humble way, we shall stand by you with a devotion that no foreigner can approach, ready to lay down our lives, if need be, in defense of yours, interlacing our industrial, commercial, civil, and religious life with yours in a way that shall make the interests of both races one. In all things that are purely social, we can be as separate as the fingers, yet one as the hand in all things essential to mutual progress.

There is no defense or security for any of us except in the highest intelligence and development of all. If anywhere there are efforts tending to curtail the fullest growth of the Negro, let these efforts be turned into stimulating, encouraging, and making him the most useful and intelligent citizen. Effort or means so invested will pay a thousand per-cent interest. These efforts will be twice blessed—blessing him that gives and him that takes. There is no escape through law of man or God from the inevitable:

> *The laws of changeless justice*
> *Bind oppressor with oppressed;*
> *And close as sin and suffering joined*
> *We march to fate abreast.*

Nearly sixteen millions of hands will aid you in pulling the load upward, or they will pull against you the load downward. We shall constitute one-third and more of the ignorance and crime of the South, or one-third its intelligence and progress; we shall contribute one-third to the business and industrial prosperity of the South, or we shall prove a veritable body of death, stagnating, depressing, retarding every effort to advance the body politic.

Gentlemen of the Exposition, as we present to you our humble effort at an exhibition of our progress, you must not expect overmuch. Starting thirty years ago with ownership here and there in a few quilts and pump-kins and chickens (gathered from miscellaneous sources), remember the path that has led from these to the inventions and production of agricul-tural implements, buggies, steam-engines, newspapers, books, statuary, carvings, paintings, the management of drugstores and banks, has not been trodden without contact with thorns and thistles.

While we take pride in what we exhibit as a result of our independent efforts, we do not for a moment forget that our part in this exhibition would fall far short of your expectations but for the constant help that has come to our educational life, not only from the Southern states, but especially from Northern philanthropists, who have made their gifts a constant stream of blessing and encouragement.

The wisest among my race understand that the agitation of questions of social equality is the extremest folly, and that progress in the enjoyment of all the privileges that will come to us must be the result of severe and constant struggle rather than of artificial forcing. No race that has anything to contribute to the markets of the world is long in any degree ostracized. It is important and right that all privileges of the law be ours, but it is vastly more important that we be prepared for the exercises of these privileges. The opportunity to earn a dollar in a factory just now is worth infinitely more than the opportunity to spend a dollar in an opera-house.

In conclusion, may I repeat that nothing in thirty years has given us more hope and encouragement, and drawn us so near to you of the white race, as this opportunity offered by the Exposition; and here bending, as it were, over the altar that represents the results of the struggles of your race and mine, both starting practically empty-handed three decades ago, I pledge that in your effort to work out the great and intricate problem which God has laid at the doors of the South, you shall have at all times the patient, sympathetic help of my race; only let this be constantly in mind, that, while from representations in these buildings of the product of field, of forest, of mine, of factory, letters, and art, much good will come, yet far above and beyond material benefits will be that higher good, that, let us pray God, will come, in a blotting out of sectional differences and racial animosities and suspicions, in a determination to administer absolute justice, in a willing obedience among all classes to the mandates of law.

This, coupled with our material prosperity, will bring into our beloved South a new heaven and a new earth.

W. E. B. Du Bois

(1868–1963)

TO THE NATIONS OF THE WORLD

July 25, 1900

W. E. B. Du Bois was born and raised in Great Barrington, Massachusetts. He received his undergraduate degree from Fisk University in Nashville, Tennessee, and his Ph.D. from Harvard. A professor at Atlanta University, Du Bois built his career as a civil rights advocate by publishing numerous books on race relations and by playing important roles in the founding of the Niagara Movement, the NAACP, and the civil rights magazine The Crisis. *A staunch opponent of the more accommodating ideology of Booker T. Washington, Du Bois firmly believed that civil rights progress was possible only through protest and agitation. The following speech was delivered by Du Bois at the First Pan-African Conference, at Westminster Hall, London.*

IN THE metropolis of the modern world, in this the closing year of the nineteenth century, there has been assembled a congress of men and women of African blood, to deliberate solemnly upon the present situation and outlook of the darker races of mankind. The problem of the twentieth century is the problem of the color line, the question as to how far differences of race—which show themselves chiefly in the color of the skin and the texture of the hair—will hereafter be made the basis of denying to over half the world the right of sharing to their utmost ability the opportunities and privileges of modern civilization.

To be sure, the darker races are today the least advanced in culture according to European standards. This has not, however, always been the case in the past, and certainly the world's history, both ancient and modern, has given many instances of no despicable ability and capacity among the blackest races of men.

In any case, the modern world must remember that in this age when the ends of the world are being brought so near together the millions of black men in Africa, America and the Islands of the Sea, not to speak of the brown and yellow myriads elsewhere, are bound to have a great influence upon the world in the future, by reason of sheer numbers and physical contact. If now the world of culture bends itself towards giving Negroes and other dark men the largest and broadest opportunity for education and self-development, then this contact and influence is bound to have a beneficial effect upon the world and hasten human progress. But if, by reason of carelessness, prejudice, greed and injustice, the black world is to be exploited and ravished and degraded, the results must be deplorable, if not fatal—not simply to them, but to the high ideals of justice, freedom and culture which a thousand years of Christian civilization have held before Europe.

And now, therefore, to these ideals of civilization, to the broader humanity of the followers of the Prince of Peace, we, the men and women of Africa in world congress assembled, do now solemnly appeal:

Let the world take no backward step in that slow but sure progress which has successively refused to let the spirit of class, of caste, of privilege, or of birth, debar from life, liberty and the pursuit of happiness a striving human soul.

Let not color or race be a feature of distinction between white and black men, regardless of worth or ability.

Let not the natives of Africa be sacrificed to the greed of gold, their liberties taken away, their family life debauched, their just aspirations repressed, and avenues of advancement and culture taken from them.

Let not the cloak of Christian missionary enterprise be allowed in the future, as so often in the past, to hide the ruthless economic exploitation and political downfall of less developed nations, whose chief fault has been reliance on the plighted faith of the Christian church.

Let the British nation, the first modern champion of Negro freedom, hasten to crown the work of Wilberforce, and Clarkson, and Buxton, and Sharpe, Bishop Colenso, and Livingstone, and give, as soon as practicable, the rights of responsible government to the black colonies of Africa and the West Indies.

Let not the spirit of Garrison, Phillips, and Douglass wholly die out in America; may the conscience of a great nation rise and rebuke all dishonesty and unrighteous oppression toward the American Negro, and grant to him the right of franchise, security of person and property, and generous recognition of the great work he has accomplished in a generation toward raising nine millions of human beings from slavery to manhood.

Let the German Empire, and the French Republic, true to their great past, remember that the true worth of colonies lies in their prosperity and progress, and that justice, impartial alike to black and white, is the first element of prosperity.

Let the Congo Free State become a great central Negro state of the world, and let its prosperity be counted not simply in cash and commerce, but in the happiness and true advancement of its black people.

Let the nations of the world respect the integrity and independence of the free Negro states of Abyssinia, Liberia, Haiti, and the rest, and let the inhabitants of these states, the independent tribes of Africa, the Negroes of the West Indies and America, and the black subjects of all nations take courage, strive ceaselessly, and fight bravely, that they may prove to the world their incontestable right to be counted among the great brotherhood of mankind.

Thus we appeal with boldness and confidence to the Great Powers of the civilized world, trusting in the wide spirit of humanity, and the deep sense of justice of our age, for a generous recognition of the righteousness of our cause.

Mary Church Terrell

(1863–1954)

WHAT IT MEANS TO BE COLORED IN THE CAPITAL OF THE UNITED STATES

October 10, 1906

The daughter of two prominent Memphis business owners who were ex-slaves, Mary Church Terrell received bachelor's and master's degrees from Oberlin College, Ohio. Throughout the course of her career as a social activist, Terrell was an educator, an author, and the cofounder and first president of the National Association of Colored Women. Terrell gave the following speech at the United Women's Club, in Washington, D.C.

THANK YOU VERY MUCH.

Washington, D.C., has been called "The Colored Man's Paradise." Whether this sobriquet was given to the national capital in bitter irony by a member of the handicapped race, as he reviewed some of his own persecutions and rebuffs, or whether it was given immediately after the war by an ex-slaveholder who for the first time in his life saw colored people walking about like free men, minus the overseer and his whip, history saith not. It is certain that it would be difficult to find a worse misnomer for Washington than "The Colored Man's Paradise" if so prosaic a consideration as veracity is to determine the appropriateness of a name.

For fifteen years I have resided in Washington, and while it was far from being a paradise for colored people when I first touched these shores it has been doing its level best ever since to make conditions for us intolerable. As a colored woman I might enter Washington any night, a stranger in a strange land, and walk miles without finding a place to lay my head. Unless I happened to know colored people who live here or ran across a chance acquaintance who could recommend a colored boarding-house to me, I should be obliged to spend the entire night

88

wandering about. Indians, Chinamen, Filipinos, Japanese and representatives of any other dark race can find hotel accommodations, if they can pay for them. The colored man alone is thrust out of the hotels of the national capital like a leper.

As a colored woman I may walk from the Capitol to the White House, ravenously hungry and abundantly supplied with money with which to purchase a meal, without finding a single restaurant in which I would be permitted to take a morsel of food, if it was patronized by white people, unless I were willing to sit behind a screen. As a colored woman I cannot visit the tomb of the Father of this country, which owes its very existence to the love of freedom in the human heart and which stands for equal opportunity to all, without being forced to sit in the Jim Crow section of an electric car which starts from the very heart of the city—midway between the Capitol and the White House. If I refuse thus to be humiliated, I am cast into jail and forced to pay a fine for violating the Virginia laws. . . .

As a colored woman I may enter more than one white church in Washington without receiving that welcome which as a human being I have the right to expect in the sanctuary of God . . .

Unless I am willing to engage in a few menial occupations, in which the pay for my services would be very poor, there is no way for me to earn an honest living, if I am not a trained nurse or a dressmaker or can secure a position as teacher in the public schools, which is exceedingly difficult to do. It matters not what my intellectual attainments may be or how great is the need of the services of a competent person, if I try to enter many of the numerous vocations in which my white sisters are allowed to engage, the door is shut in my face.

From one Washington theater I am excluded altogether. In the remainder certain seats are set aside for colored people, and it is almost impossible to secure others . . .

With the exception of the Catholic University, there is not a single white college in the national capital to which colored people are admitted. . . . A few years ago the Columbian Law School admitted colored students, but in deference to the Southern white students the authorities have decided to exclude them altogether.

Some time ago a young woman who had already attracted some attention in the literary world by her volume of short stories answered an advertisement which appeared in a Washington newspaper, which called for the services of a skilled stenographer and expert typewriter. . . . The applicants were requested to send specimens of their work and answer certain questions concerning their experience and their speed before they called in person. In reply to her application the young colored woman . . . received a letter from the firm stating that her references and experience were the most satisfactory that had been sent and requesting her to call. When she presented herself there was some doubt in the mind of the man to whom she was directed concerning her racial pedigree, so he asked her point-blank whether she was colored or white. When she confessed the truth the merchant expressed . . . deep regret that he could not avail himself of the services of so competent a person, but frankly admitted that employing a colored woman in his establishment in any except a menial position was simply out of the question. . . .

Not only can colored women secure no employment in the Washington stores, department and otherwise, except as menials, and such positions, of course, are few, but even as customers they are not infrequently treated with discourtesy both by the clerks and the proprietor himself. . . .

Although white and colored teachers are under the same Board of Education and the system for the children of both races is said to be uniform, prejudice against the colored teachers in the public schools is manifested in a variety of ways. From 1870 to 1900 there was a colored superintendent at the head of the colored schools. During all that time the directors of the cooking, sewing, physical culture, manual training, music and art departments were colored people. Six years ago a change was inaugurated. The colored superintendent was legislated out of office and the directorships, without a single exception, were taken from colored teachers and given to the whites. . . .

Now, no matter how competent or superior the colored teachers in our public schools may be, they know that they can never rise to the height of a directorship, can never hope to be more than an assistant and receive the meager salary therefore, unless the present regime is radically changed. . . .

Strenuous efforts are being made to run Jim Crow cars in the national capital. . . . Representative Heflin, of Alabama, who introduced a bill providing for Jim Crow street cars in the District of Columbia last winter, has just received a letter from the president of the East Brookland Citizens' Association "indorsing the movement for separate street cars and sincerely hoping that you will be successful in getting this enacted into a law as soon as possible." Brookland is a suburb of Washington.

The colored laborer's path to a decent livelihood is by no means smooth. Into some of the trades unions here he is admitted, while from others he is excluded altogether. By the union men this is denied, although I am personally acquainted with skilled workmen who tell me they are not admitted into the unions because they are colored. But even when they are allowed to join the unions they frequently derive little benefit, owing to certain tricks of the trade. When the word passes round that help is needed and colored laborers apply, they are often told by the union officials that they have secured all the men they needed, because the places are reserved for white men, until they have been provided with jobs, and colored men must remain idle, unless the supply of white men is too small. . . .

And so I might go on citing instance after instance to show the variety of ways in which our people are sacrificed on the altar of prejudice in the Capital of the United States and how almost insurmountable are the obstacles which block his path to success. . . .

It is impossible for any white person in the United States, no matter how sympathetic and broad, to realize what life would mean to him if his incentive to effort were suddenly snatched away. To the lack of incentive to effort, which is the awful shadow under which we live, may be traced the wreck and ruin of score of colored youth. And surely nowhere in the world do oppression and persecution based solely on the color of the skin appear more hateful and hideous than in the capital of the United States, because the chasm between the principles upon which this Government was founded, in which it still professes to believe, and those which are daily practiced under the protection of the flag, yawn so wide and deep.

Francis J. Grimké

(1850–1937)

EQUALITY OF RIGHTS FOR ALL CITIZENS: BLACK AND WHITE, ALIKE

March 7, 1909

Francis J. Grimké was born in Charleston, South Carolina, the son of plantation owner Henry Grimké and a slave. Francis was educated at Howard University and at the Princeton Theological Seminary. He became a renowned Presbyterian minister, and was one of eighteen scholars responsible for the creation of the American Negro Academy (1897). Grimké delivered the following address at the Fifteenth Street Presbyterian Church, in Washington, D.C.

I Cor. 16:13. "Watch ye, stand fast in
the faith, quit you like men, be strong."

IT HAS been my custom for many years to speak during the inaugural week on some phase of the race question. I have done it because usually at such times there are representatives of our race here from all parts of the country, and an opportunity is thus afforded of reaching a larger number than would be possible at any other time. Such occasions, it seems to me, should be utilized in the interest of the race, in the discussion of matters pertaining to the race. The inauguration of a President is an event in which the whole nation is interested, and which emphasizes the fact of citizenship, as perhaps nothing else does, coming as it does after the election, and growing out of it. On such occasions it is well for us, therefore, especially at this juncture of our history, not to be unmindful of our own citizenship, of our own status in the body politic.

We have just been celebrating, all over the country, the centennial of the birth of Abraham Lincoln, our great war President, and this inauguration coming so soon after, makes it especially a good time to talk about some of the questions which grew out of the war, and which were settled by it. And this is what I want to do this morning.

Over forty years ago the great struggle ended, the "irrepressible conflict" came to a close. It marked an epoch in the history of our country, and in the history of the black race in this country. Certain great questions, which had agitated the country for years, were settled, and settled for all time.

* * * * *

It is now no longer a question as to whether we are a nation, or a confederation of sovereign and independent States. That question is settled, and settled once for all by the issue of the War. It is not likely that any Southern State will ever again attempt to withdraw from the Union, or to act on the assumption that it has the right to do so. Even if it is foolish enough to entertain such a view, it will be sure never again to act upon it. The issue of the War has removed forever from the field of serious discussion this question of the right of a State to secede. The ghost of secession will never again arise to disturb the peace of the Union. The Stars and Stripes, the old flag, will float, as long as it floats, over all these States, from the Atlantic to the Pacific, from the Lakes to the Gulf. If the time ever comes when we shall go to pieces, it will not be from any desire or disposition on the part of the States to pull apart, but from inward corruption, from the disregard of right principles, from the spirit of greed, from the narrowing lust of gold, from losing sight of the fact that "righteousness exalteth a nation, but that sin is a reproach to any people." It is here where our real danger lies—not in the secession of States from the Union, but in the secession of the Union itself from the great and immutable principles of right, of justice, of fair play for all regardless of race, color, or previous condition of servitude. The fact that the Union has been saved, that these rebellious States have been brought back into it, will amount to nothing unless it can be saved from this still greater peril that threatens it. The secession of the Southern States in 1860 was a small matter compared with the secession of the Union itself from the great principles enunciated in the Declaration of Independence, in the Golden Rule, in the Ten Commandments, in the Sermon on the Mount. Unless we hold, and hold firmly to these great fundamental principles of righteousness, of social, political, and economic wisdom, our Union, as Mr. Garrison expressed it, will be "only a covenant with death and an agreement with hell." If it continues to exist it will be a curse, and not a blessing.

Our brave boys in blue, whose bodies lie moldering in the grave, but whose souls are marching on, settled the question of the Union of the States. It is for the patriotic men who are living to-day, and those who are to follow in their footsteps, to deal with this larger and more important question. It isn't enough that these States are held together, they must be held together on right principles—principles of justice, of equity, of fair play, of equality before the law for all alike. Whether there is patriotism, political wisdom, moral insight and stamina enough to lead men to forget their differences on minor matters and to unite their forces for the attainment of this greater and more important end, remains to be seen. There are so many who are controlled by their petty prejudices, whose views are so narrow and contracted, that they seem incapable of appreciating the things of prime importance, the things that are fundamental in the life of the nation, and upon which its future and peace and prosperity depend. The fear of rebellion is forever gone. It is not so, however, with regard to the danger of which I am speaking—the danger of the nation divorcing itself from sound political and moral principles.

* * * * *

In the scheme of citizenship of our country for years following the close of the war the Negro had no part; and he had no part because he was looked upon as an inferior. "Subordination to the superior race is declared to be his natural and moral condition." His inferiority was asserted to be a "great physical, philosophical, and moral truth."

And this is exactly the Southern view to-day; and is exactly the programme to which it is committed. Its whole attitude to-day is in harmony with the great principle upon which the Southern Confederacy was founded—the non-recognition of the Negro as an equal in any respect—socially, civilly, politically. The South holds to this view just as tenaciously to-day as it did when Mr. Stephens made his Great Cornerstone Speech in 1861. The Ku Klux Klan, the White Caps, the Red Shirt Brigade, tissue ballots, the revised constitutions with their grandfather clauses, Jim Crow Car legislation, the persistent effort of the South to disfranchise the Negro—all these things have grown out of the idea that the rightful place of the Negro is that of subordination to the white man, that he has no rightful place in the body politic.

* * * * *

But I cannot believe that the nation is always going to leave its loyal black citizens to be despoiled of their civil and political rights by the men who sought to destroy the Union. A better day is coming, and coming soon, I trust.

While we are waiting, however, for the nation to come to its senses—waiting for a revival of the spirit of justice and of true democracy in the land—it is important for us to remember that much, very much, will depend upon ourselves. In the passage of Scripture read in our hearing at the beginning of this discourse, three things we are exhorted to do, and must do, if we are ever to secure our rights in this land: We are exhorted to be watchful. "Watch ye," is the exhortation. We are to be on our guard. "Eternal vigilance is the price of liberty." There are enemies ever about us and they are ever plotting our ruin—enemies within the race and without it. We have got to live in the consciousness of this fact. If we assume that all is well, that there is nothing to fear, and so relax our vigilance, so cease to be watchful, we need not be surprised if our enemies get the better of us, if we are worsted in the conflict.

(2) We are exhorted to stand fast in the faith. In the faith we feel that, as American citizens, we are entitled to the same rights and privileges as other citizens of the Republic. In this faith we are to stand, and stand fast. We are not to give it up; we are not to allow anyone, white or black, friend or foe, to induce us to retreat a single inch from this position.

(3) We are exhorted to quit ourselves like men, to be strong. And by this, I understand, is meant that we are to stand up in a manly way for our rights; that we are to seek by every honorable means the full enjoyment of our rights. It is still true—

"Who would be free himself must strike the blow."

And, if we are ever to be free from invidious distinctions in this country, based upon race, color, previous condition, we have got to be alive, wide-awake to our own interest. If we are not, we have no right to expect others to be; we have no right to expect anything but failure, but defeat. And we deserve defeat if ours is the spirit of indifference, of unconcern. We are not going to secure our rights in this land without a struggle. We have got to contend, and contend earnestly, for what belongs to us. Victory isn't coming in any other way. No silent acquiescence on our part in the wrongs from which we are suffering, contrary to law; no giving of ourselves merely to the work of improving our condition, materially, intellectually, morally, spiritually, however zealously pursued, is going to bring relief. We have got, in addition to the effort we are making to improve ourselves, to keep up the agitation, and keep it up until right triumphs and wrong is put down. A programme of silence on the part of the race is a fool's programme. Reforms, changes in public sentiment, the righting of wrongs, are never effected in that way; and our wrongs will never be. A race that sits quietly down and rests in sweet content in the midst of the wrongs from which it is suffering is not worth contending for, is not worth saving.

This is not true of this race, however. We are not sitting down in sweet content, let it be said to our credit. I thank God from the bottom of my heart for these mutterings of discontent that are heard in all parts of the land. The fact that we are dissatisfied with present conditions, and that we are becoming more and more so, shows that we are growing in manhood, in self-respect, in the qualities that will enable us to win out in the end. It is our duty to keep up the agitation for our rights, not only for our sakes, but also for the sake of the nation at large. It would not only be against our own interest not to do so, but it would be unpatriotic for us quietly to acquiesce in the present condition of things, for it is a wrong condition of things. If justice sleeps in this land, let it not be because we have helped to lull it to sleep by our silence, our indifference; let it not be from lack of effort on our part to arouse it from its slumbers. Elijah said to the prophets of Baal, while they were crying to the god, "Peradventure he sleepeth." And it may be that he was asleep; but it was not their fault that he continued asleep, for they kept up a continual uproar about his altar. And so here, sleeping Justice in this land may go on slumbering, but let us see to it that it is due to no fault of ours. Even Baalam's ass cried out in protest when smitten by his brutal master, and God gave him the power to cry out, endowed him miraculously with speech in which to voice his protest.

It is not necessary for God to work a miracle to enable us to protest against our wrong; He has already given us the power. Let us see to it that we use it. If we are wise we will be able to take care of ourselves. If we are not wise, however, if we adopt the policy of silence, and if we continue to feel that it is our duty to follow blindly, slavishly, any one political party, we will receive only such treatment as is accorded to slaves, and will go on pleading for our rights in vain. The only wise course for us to pursue is to keep on agitating, and to cast our votes where they will tell most for the race. As to what party we affiliate with is a matter of no importance whatever; the important thing is our rights. And until we recognize that fact, and act upon it, we will be the football of all political parties. John Boyle O'Reilly, in speaking on the race question years ago, said: "If I were a colored man I should use parties as I would a club— to break down prejudice against my people. I shouldn't talk about being true to any party, except so far as that party was true to me. Parties care nothing for you, only to use you. You should use parties; the highest party you have in this country is your own manhood. That is the thing in danger from all parties; that is the thing that every colored man is bound in duty to himself and his children to defend and protect." And that is good advice. It embodies the highest political wisdom for us as a people.

The exhortation of the text is, "Watch ye, stand fast in the faith, quit you like men, be strong." And this is the message that I bring to you, who are here this morning, and to the members of our race all over the country. We must be watchful; we must hold firmly to our faith in our citizenship, and in our rights as citizens; and we must act the part of men in the maintenance of those rights. In the end the victory is sure to be ours. The right is bound, sooner or later, to triumph.

> "Before the monstrous wrong he sits him down—
> One man against a stone-walled city of sin.
> For centuries those walls have been a-building;
> Smooth porphyry, they slope and coldly glass
> The flying storm and wheeling sun.

> "No chinks, no crevice, lets the thinnest arrow in.
> He fights alone, and from the cloudy ramparts
> A thousand evil faces gibe and jeer him.
> Let him lie down and die; what is the right
> And where is justice in a world like this?

> "But by and by earth shakes herself, impatient;
> And down, in one great roar of ruin, crash
> Watch-tower and citadel and battlements.
> When the red dust has cleared, the lonely soldier
> Stands with strange thoughts beneath the friendly stars."

And so, in the end, will it be with this great evil of race prejudice against which we are contending in this country, if, like the lonely soldier, we show the same earnestness, the same patient determination, the same invincible courage. A better day is coming; but we have got to help to bring it about. It isn't coming independently of our efforts, and it isn't coming by quietly, timidly, cowardly acquiescing in our wrongs.

Ida B. Wells–Barnett

(1862–1931)

THIS AWFUL SLAUGHTER

May 8, 1909

Born to slaves, Ida B. Wells-Barnett was educated at Rust University in Mississippi and Fisk University in Tennessee, before going on to a much lauded career as a journalist. Over the course of her career, Wells-Barnett wrote for the Memphis Free Speech *(of which she was part owner), the* Chicago Conservator *and the* New York Age, *making a name for herself through her one-woman journalistic crusade against lynching. The following speech was delivered at the NAACP's first annual conference in Atlanta, Georgia.*

THE LYNCHING record for a quarter of a century merits the thoughtful study of the American people. It presents three salient facts:

First, lynching is color-line murder. Second, crimes against women is the excuse, not the cause. Third, it is a national crime and requires a national remedy.

Proof that lynching follows the color line is to be found in the statistics which have been kept for the past twenty-five years. During the few years preceding this period and while frontier law existed, the executions showed a majority of white victims. Later, however, as law courts and authorized judiciary extended into the far West, lynch law rapidly abated, and its white victims became few and far between.

Just as the lynch-law regime came to a close in the West, a new mob movement started in the South. This was wholly political, its purpose being to suppress the colored vote by intimidation and murder. Thousands of assassins banded together under the name of Ku Klux Klans, "Midnight Raiders," "Knights of the Golden Circle," et cetera, et cetera, spread a reign of terror, by beating, shooting and killing colored people by the thousands. In a few years, the purpose was accomplished, and the black vote was supressed. But mob murder continued.

From 1882, in which year fifty-two were lynched, down to the present, lynching has been along the color line. Mob murder increased yearly until in 1892 more than two hundred victims were lynched and statistics show tht 3,284 men, women and children have been put to death in this quarter of a century. During the last ten years from 1899 to 1908 inclusive the number lynched was 959. Of this number 102 were white, while the colored victims numbered 857. No other nation, civilized or savage, burns its criminals; only under that Stars and Stripes is the human holocaust possible. Twenty-eight human beings burned at the stake, one of them a woman and two of them children, is the awful indictment against American civilization—the gruesome tribute which the nation pays to the color line.

Why is mob murder permitted by a Christian nation? What is the cause of this awful slaughter? This question is answered almost daily—always the same shameless falsehood that "Negroes are lynched to protect womanhood." Standing before a Chautauqua assemblage, John Temple Graves, at once champion of lynching and apologist for lynchers, said: "The mob stands today as the most potential bulwark between the women of the South and such a carnival of crime as would infuriate the world and precipitate the annihilation of the Negro race." This is the never-varying answer of lynchers and their apologists. All know that it is untrue. The cowardly lyncher revels in murder, then seeks to shield himself from public execration by claiming devotion to woman. But truth is mighty and the lynching record discloses the hypocrisy of the lyncher as well as his crime.

The Springfield, Illinois, mob rioted for two days, the militia of the entire state was called out, two men were lynched, hundreds of people driven from their homes, all because a white woman said a Negro assaulted her. A mad mob went to the jail, tried to lynch the victim of her charge and, not being able to find him, proceeded to pillage and burn the town and to lynch two innocent men. Later, after the police had found that the woman's charge was false, she published a retraction, the indictment was dismissed and the intended victim discharged. But the lynched victims were dead. Hundreds were homeless and Illinois was disgraced.

As a final and complete refutation of the charge that lynching is occasioned by crimes against women, a partial record of lynchings is cited; 285 persons were lynched for causes as follows:

Unknown cause, 92; no cause, 10; race prejudice, 49; miscegenation, 7; informing, 12; making threats, 11; keeping saloon, 3; practicing fraud, 5;

practicing voodooism, 2; bad reputation, 8; unpopularity, 3; mistaken identity, 5; using improper language, 3; violation of contract, 1; writing insulting letter, 2; eloping, 2; poisoning horse, 1; poisoning well, 2; by white caps, 9; vigilantes, 14; Indians, 1; moonshining, 1; refusing evidence, 2; political causes, 5; disputing, 1; disobeying quarantine regulations, 2; slapping a child, 1; turning state's evidence, 3; protecting a Negro, 1; to prevent giving evidence, 1; knowledge of larceny, 1; writing letter to white woman, 1; asking white woman to marry, 1; jilting girl, 1; having smallpox, 1; concealing criminal, 2; threatening political exposure, 1; self-defense, 6; cruelty, 1; insulting language to woman, 5; quarreling with white man, 2; colonizing Negroes, 1; throwing stones, 1; quarreling, 1; gambling, 1.

Is there a remedy, or will the nation confess that it cannot protect its protectors at home as well as abroad? Various remedies have been suggested to abolish the lynching infamy, but year after year, the butchery of men, women and children continues in spite of plea and protest. Education is suggested as a preventive, but it is as grave a crime to murder an ignorant man as it is a scholar. True, few educated men have been lynched, but the hue and cry once started stops at no bounds, as was clearly shown by the lynchings in Atlanta, and in Springfield, Illinois.

Agitation, though helpful, will not alone stop the crime. Year after year statistics are published, meetings are held, resolutions are adopted and yet lynchings go on. Public sentiment does measurably decrease the sway of mob law, but the irresponsible bloodthirsty criminals who swept through the streets of Springfield, beating an inoffensive law-abiding citizen to death in one part of the town, and in another torturing and shooting to death a man who for threescore years had made a reputation for honesty, integrity and sobriety, had raised a family and had accumulated property, were not deterred from their heinous crimes by either education or agitation.

The only certain remedy is an appeal to law. Lawbreakers must be made to know that human life is sacred and that every citizen of this country is first a citizen of the United States and secondly a citizen of the state in which he belongs. This nation must assert itself and protect its federal citizenship at home as well as abroad. The strong arm of the government must reach across state lines whenever unbridled lawlessness defies state laws and must give to the individual under the Stars and Stripes the same measure of protection it gives to him when he travels in foreign lands.

Federal protection of American citizenship is the remedy for lynching. Foreigners are rarely lynched in America. If, by mistake, one is lynched, the national government quickly pays the damages. The recent agitation in California against the Japanese compelled this nation to recognize that federal power must yet assert itself to protect the nation from the treason of sovereign states. Thousands of American citizens have been put to death and no President has yet raised his hand in effective protest, but a simple insult to a native of Japan was quite sufficient to stir the government at Washington to prevent the threatened wrong. If the government has power to protect a foreigner from insult, certainly it has power to save a citizen's life.

The practical remedy has been more than once suggested in Congress. Senator Gallinger, of New Hampshire, in a resolution introduced in Congress called for an investigation "with the view of ascertaining whether there is a remedy for lynching which Congress may apply." The Senate Committee has under consideration a bill drawn by A. E. Pillsbury, formerly Attorney General of Massachusetts, providing for federal prosecution of lynchers in cases where the state fails to protect citizens or foreigners. Both of these resolutions indicate that the attention of the nation has been called to this phase of the lynching question.

As a final word, it would be a beginning in the right direction if this conference can see its way clear to establish a bureau for the investigation and publication of the details of every lynching, so that the public could know that an influential body of citizens has made it a duty to give the widest publicity to the facts in each case; that it will make an effort to secure expressions of opinion all over the country against lynching for the sake of the country's fair name; and lastly, but by no means least, to try to influence the daily papers of the country to refuse to become accessory to mobs either before or after the fact.

Several of the greatest riots and most brutal burnt offerings of the mobs have been suggested and incited by the daily papers of the offending community. If the newspaper which suggests lynching in its accounts of an alleged crime, could be held legally as well as morally responsible for reporting that "threats of lynching were heard"; or, "it is feared that if the guilty one is caught, he will be lynched"; or, "there were cries of 'lynch him,' and the only reason the threat was not carried out was because no leader appeared," a long step toward a remedy will have been taken.

In a multitude of counsel there is wisdom. Upon the grave question presented by the slaughter of innocent men, women and children there should be an honest, courageous conference of patriotic, law-abiding citizens anxious to punish crime promptly, impartially and by due process of law, also to make life, liberty and property secure against mob rule.

Time was when lynching appeared to be sectional, but now it is national—a blight upon our nation, mocking our laws and disgracing our Christianity. "With malice toward none but with charity for all" let us undertake the work of making the "law of the land" effective and supreme upon every foot of American soil—a shield to the innocent; and to the guilty, punishment swift and sure.

Marcus Garvey

(1887–1940)

THE PRINCIPLES OF THE UNIVERSAL
NEGRO IMPROVEMENT ASSOCIATION
November 25, 1922

Born and raised on the island of Jamaica, Marcus Garvey first gained the public eye when he founded the Universal Negro Improvement Association and African Communities League in Jamaica in 1914. Upon hearing of the organization, Booker T. Washington invited Garvey to the United States in hopes of their working together. Unfortunately, Washington died before Garvey's arrival. Nonetheless, Marcus Garvey did organize a chapter of the UNIA in the United States, using his platform to become one of the twentieth century's most influential and controversial civil rights leaders.

OVER FIVE years ago the Universal Negro Improvement Association placed itself before the world as the movement through which the new and rising Negro would give expression of his feelings. This Association adopts an attitude not of hostility to other races and peoples of the world, but an attitude of self-respect, of manhood rights on behalf of 400,000,000 Negroes of the world.

We represent peace, harmony, love, human sympathy, human rights and human justice, and that is why we fight so much. Wheresoever human rights are denied to any group, wheresoever justice is denied to any group, there the U.N.I.A. finds a cause. And at this time among all the peoples of the world, the group that suffers most from injustice, the group that is denied most of those rights that belong to all humanity is the black group of 400,000,000. Because of that injustice, because of that denial of our rights, we go forth under the leadership of the One who is always on the side of right to fight the common cause of humanity; to fight as we fought in the Revolutionary War, as we fought in the Civil War, as we fought in the Spanish-American War, and as we fought in the war between 1914–1918 on the battle plains of France and Flanders. As we fought up the heights of Mesopotamia; even so under the leadership of the U.N.I.A., we are marshaling the 400,000,000 Negroes of the world to fight for the emancipation of the race and of the redemption of the country of our fathers.

We represent a new line of thought among Negroes. Whether you call it advanced thought or reactionary thought, I do not care. If it is reactionary for people to seek independence in government, then we are reactionary. If it is advanced though for people to seek liberty and freedom, then we represent the advanced school of thought among the Negroes of this country. We of the U.N.I.A. believe that what is good for the other fellow is good for us. If government is something that is worthwhile; if government is something that is appreciable and helpful and protective to others, then we also want to experiment in government. We do not mean a government that will make us citizens without rights or subjects without considerations. We mean the kind of government that will place our race in control, even as other races are in control of their own governments.

That does not suggest anything that is unreasonable. It was not unreasonable for George Washington, the great hero and father of the country, to have fought for the freedom of America giving to us this great republic and this great democracy; it was not unreasonable for the Liberals of France to have fought against the Monarchy to give to the world French Democracy and French Republicanism; it was no unrighteous cause that led Tolstoy to sound the call of liberty in Russia, which has ended in giving to the world the social democracy of Russia, an experiment that will probably prove to be a boon and a blessing to mankind. If it was not an unrighteous cause that led Washington to fight for the independence of this country, and led the Liberals of France to establish the Republic, it is therefore not an unrighteous cause for the U.N.I.A. to lead 400,000,000 Negroes all over the world to fight for the liberation of our country.

Therefore U.N.I.A. is not advocating the cause of church building, because we have a sufficiently large number of churches among us to minister to the spiritual needs of the people, and we are not going to compete with those who are engaged in so splendid a work; we are not engaged in building any new social institutions, and Y.M.C.A.'s or Y.W.C.A.'s because there are enough social workers engaged in those praise-worthy efforts. We are not engaged in politics because we have enough local politicians, Democrats, Socialists, Soviets, etc., and the political situation is well taken care of. We are not engaged in domestic politics, in church building or in social uplift work, but we are engaged in nation building.

In advocating the principles of this Association we find we have been very much misunderstood and very much misrepresented by men from within our own race, as well as others from without. Any reform movement that seeks to bring about changes for the benefit of humanity is bound to be misrepresented by those who have always taken it upon themselves to administer to, and lead the unfortunate, and to direct those who may be placed under temporary disadvantages. It has been so in all other movements whether social or political; hence those of us in the Universal Negro Improvement Association who lead do not feel in any way embarrassed about this misrepresentation, about this misunderstanding as far as the Aims and Objects of the Negro Improvement Association go. But those who probably would have taken kindly notice of this great movement, have been led to believe that this movement seeks, not to develop the good within the race, but to give expression to that which is most destructive and most harmful to society and to government.

I desire to remove the misunderstanding that has been created in the minds of millions of peoples throughout the world in their relationship to the organization. The Universal Negro Improvement Association stands for the bigger brotherhood; the Universal Negro Improvement Association stands for human rights, not only for Negroes, but for all races. The Universal Negro Improvement Association believes in the rights of not only the black race, but the white race, the yellow race and the brown race. The Universal Negro Improvement Association believes that the white man has as much right to be considered, the yellow man has as much right to be considered, the brown man has as much right to be considered as well as the black man of Africa. In view of the fact that the black man of Africa has contributed as much to the world as the white man of Europe, and the brown man and yellow man of Asia, we of the Universal Negro Improvement Association demand that the white, yellow and brown races give to the black man his place in the civilization of the world. We ask for nothing more than the rights of 400,000,000 Negroes. We are not seeking, as I said before, to destroy or disrupt the society or the government of other races, but we are determined that 400,000,000 of us shall unite ourselves to free our motherland from the grasp of the invader. We of the Universal Negro Improvement Association are determined to unite 400,000,000 Negroes for their own industrial, political, social and religious emancipation.

We of the Universal Negro Improvement Association are determined to unite the 400,000,000 Negroes of the world to give expression to their own feeling; we are determined to unite the 400,000,000 Negroes of the world for the purpose of building a civilization of their own. And in that effort we desire to bring together the 15,000,000 of the United States, the 180,000,000 in Asia, in the West Indies and Central and South America, and the 200,000,000 in Africa. We are looking toward political freedom on the continent of Africa, the land of our fathers.

The Universal Negro Improvement Association is not seeking to build up another government within the bounds or borders of the United States of America. The Universal Negro Improvement Association is not seeking to disrupt any organized system of government, but the Association is determined to bring Negroes together for the building up of a nation of their own. And why? Because we have been forced to it. We have been forced to it throughout the world; not only in America, not only in Europe, not only in the British Empire, but wheresoever the black man happens to find himself, he has been forced to do for himself.

To talk about government is a little more than some of our people can appreciate just at this time. The average man does not think that way, just because he finds himself a citizen or a subject of some country. He seems to say, "Why should there be need for any other government?" We are French, English or American. But we of the U.N.I.A. have studied seriously this question of nationality among Negroes—this American nationality, this British nationality, this French, Italian or Spanish nationality, and have discovered that it counts for nought when that nationality comes in conflict with the racial idealism of the group that rules. When our interests clash with those of the ruling faction, then we find that we have absolutely no rights. In times of peace, when everything is all right, Negroes have a hard time, wherever we go, wheresoever we find ourselves, getting those rights that belong to us, in common with others whom we claim as fellow citizens; getting that consideration that should be ours by right of the constitution, by right of the law; but in the time of trouble they make us all partners in the cause, as happened in the last war, when we were partners, whether British, French or American Negroes. And we were told that we must forget everything in an effort to save the nation.

We have saved many nations in this manner, and we have lost our lives doing that before. Hundreds of thousands—nay, millions of black men, lie buried under the ground due to that old-time camouflage of saving the nation. We saved the British Empire; we saved the French Empire; we saved this glorious country more than once; and all that we have received for our sacrifices, all that we have received for what we have done, even in giving up our lives, is just what you are receiving now, just what I am receiving now.

You and I fare no better in America, in the British Empire, or in any other part of the white world; we fare no better than any black man wheresoever he shows his head. And why? Because we have been satisfied to allow ourselves to be led, educated, to be directed by the other fellow, who has always sought to lead in the world in that direction that would satisfy him and strengthen his position. We have allowed ourselves for the last 500 years to be a race of followers, following every race that has led in the direction that would make them more secure.

The U.N.I.A. is reversing the old-time order of things. We refuse to be followers any more. We are leading ourselves. That means, if any saving is to be done, later on, whether it is saving this one nation or that one government, we are going to seek a method of saving Africa first. Why? And why Africa? Because Africa has become the grand prize of the nations. Africa has become the big game of the nation hunters. Today Africa looms as the greatest commercial, industrial and political prize in the world.

The difference between the Universal Negro Improvement Association and the other movements of this country, and probably the world, is that the Universal Negro Improvement Association seeks independence of government, while the other organizations seek to make the Negro a secondary part of existing governments. We differ from the organizations in America because they seek to subordinate the Negro as a secondary consideration in a great civilization, knowing that in America the Negro will never reach his highest ambition, knowing that the Negro in America will never get his constitutional rights. All those organizations which are fostering the improvement of Negroes in the British Empire know that the Negro in the British Empire will never reach the highest of his constitutional rights. What do I mean by constitutional rights in America? If the black man is to reach the height of his ambition in this country—if the black man is to get all of his constitutional rights in America—then the black man should have the same chance in the nation as any other man to become president of the nation, or a street cleaner in New York. If the black man in the British Empire is to have all his constitutional rights it means that the Negro in the British Empire should have at least the same right to become premier of Great Britain as he has to become a street cleaner in the city of London. Are they prepared to give us such political equality? You and I can live in the United States of America for 100 or more years, and our generations may live for 200 years or for 5000 more years, and so long as there is a black and white population, when the majority is on the side of the white race, you and I will never get political justice or get political equality in this country. Then why should a black man with rising ambition, after preparing himself in every possible way to give expression to that highest ambition, allow himself to be kept down by racial prejudice within a country? If I am as educated as the next man, if I am as prepared as the next man, if I have passed through the best schools and colleges and universities as the other fellow, why should I not have a fair chance to compete with the other fellow for the biggest position in the nation? I have feelings, I have blood, I have senses like the other fellow; I have ambition, I have hope. Why should he, because of some racial prejudice, keep me down and why should I concede to him the right to rise above me, and to establish himself as my permanent master? That is where the U.N.I.A. differs from other organizations. I refuse to stultify my ambition, and every true Negro refuses to stultify his ambition to suit any one, and therefore the U.N.I.A. decides if America is not big enough for two presidents, if England is not big enough for two kings, then we are not going to quarrel over the matter; we will leave one president in America, we will leave one king in England, we will leave one president in France and we will have one president in Africa. Hence, the Universal Negro Improvement Association does not seek to interfere with the social and political systems of France, but by the arrangement of things today the U.N.I.A. refuses to recognize any political or social system in Africa except that which we are about to establish for ourselves.

We are not preaching a propaganda of hate against anybody. We love the white man; we love all humanity, because we feel that we cannot live without the other. The white man is as necessary to the existence of the Negro as the Negro is necessary to his existence. There is a common relationship that we cannot escape. Africa has certain things that Europe wants, and Europe has certain things that Africa wants, and if a fair and square deal must bring white and black with each other, it is impossible for us to escape it. Africa has oil, diamonds, copper, gold and rubber and all the minerals that Europe wants, and there must be some kind of relationship between Africa and Europe for a fair exchange, so we cannot afford to hate anybody.

The question often asked is what does it require to redeem a race and free a country? If it takes manpower, if it takes scientific intelligence, if it takes education of any kind, or if it takes blood, then the 400,000,000 Negroes of the world have it.

It took the combined manpower of the Allies to put down the mad determination of the Kaiser to impose German will upon the world and upon humanity. Among those who suppressed his mad ambition were two million Negroes who have not yet forgotten how to drive men across the firing line. Surely those of us who faced German shot and shell at the Marne, at Verdun, have not forgotten the order of our Commander-in-Chief. The cry that caused us to leave America in such mad haste, when white fellow citizens of America refused to fight and said, "We do not believe in war and therefore, even though we are American citizens, and even though the nation is in danger, we will not go to war." When many of them cried out and said, "We are German-Americans and we cannot fight," when so many white men refused to answer to the call and dodged behind all kinds of excuses, 400,000 black men were ready without a question. It was because we were told it was a war of democracy; it was a war for the liberation of the weaker peoples of the world. We heard the cry of Woodrow Wilson, not because we liked him so, but because the things he said were of such a nature that they appealed to us as men. Wheresoever the cause of humanity stands in need of assistance, there you will find the Negro ever ready to serve.

He has done it from the time of Christ up to now. When the whole world turned its back upon the Christ, the man who was said to be the Son of God; when the world cried out, "Crucify Him," when the world spurned Him and spat upon Him, it was a black man, Simon, the Cyrenian, who took up the cross. Why? Because the cause of humanity appealed to him. When the black man saw the suffering Jew, struggling under the heavy cross, he was willing to go to His assistance, and he bore that cross up to the heights of Calvary. In the spirit of Simon, the Cyrenian, 1900 years ago, we answered the call of Woodrow Wilson, the call of a larger humanity, and it was for that that we willingly rushed into the war from America, from the West Indies, over 100,000; it was for that that we rushed into the war from Africa, 2,000,000 of us. We met in France, Flanders and in Mesopotamia. We fought unfalteringly. When the white men faltered and fell back on their battle lines, at the Marne and at Verdun, when they ran away from the charge of the German hordes, the black hell fighters stood before the can-nonade, stood before the charge, and again they shouted, "There will be a hot time in the old town tonight."

We made it so hot a few months after our appearance in France and on the various battle fronts, we succeeded in driving the German hordes across the Rhine, and driving the Kaiser out of Germany, and out of Potsdam into Holland. We have not forgotten the prowess of war. If we have been liberal-minded enough to give our life's blood in France, in Mesopotamia and elsewhere, fighting for the white man, whom we have always assisted, surely we have not forgotten to fight for ourselves, and when the time comes that the world will again give Africa an opportunity for freedom, surely 400,000,000 black men will march out on the battle plains of Africa, under the colors of the red, the black and the green.

We shall march out, yes, as black American citizens, as black British subjects, as black French citizens, as black Italians or as black Spaniards, but we shall march out with a greater loyalty, the loyalty of race. We shall march out in answer to the cry of our fathers, who cry out to us for the redemption of our own country, our motherland, Africa.

We shall march out, not forgetting the blessings of America. We shall march out, not forgetting the blessings of civilization. We shall march out with a history of peace before and behind us, and surely that history shall be our breastplate, for how can man fight better than knowing that the cause for which he fights is righteous? How can man fight more gloriously than by knowing that behind him is a history of slavery, a history of bloody carnage and massacre inflicted upon a race because of its inability to pro-tect itself and fight? Shall we not fight for the glorious opportunity of pro-tecting and forevermore establishing ourselves as a mighty race and nation, nevermore to be disrespected by men. Glorious shall be the battle when the time comes to fight for our people and our race.

We should say to the millions who are in Africa to hold the fort, for we are coming 400,000,000 strong.

Mary McLeod Bethune

(1875–1955)

WHAT DOES AMERICAN DEMOCRACY MEAN TO ME?
November 23, 1939

The daughter of former slaves, Mary McLeod Bethune was educated at the Scotia Seminary in Concord, North Carolina, and the Moody Bible Institute in Chicago, Illinois. After marrying Albertus L. Bethune in 1898, Mary moved to Daytona Beach, Florida, where she later founded the Daytona Normal and Industrial Institute for Negro Girls (now known as Bethune-Cookman College). The energetic leader of numerous organizations, Mary McLeod Bethune was eventually named by Franklin D. Roosevelt as the director of the Office of Minority Affairs in the National Youth Administration (1935). The following speech by Bethune was part of a panel discussion on NBC radio, wherein the panelists were asked to speak about what American democracy meant to them.

DEMOCRACY IS for me, and for 12 million black Americans, a goal towards which our nation is marching. It is a dream and an ideal in whose ultimate realization we have a deep and abiding faith. For me, it is based on Christianity, in which we confidently entrust our destiny as a people. Under God's guidance in this great democracy, we are rising out of the darkness of slavery into the light of freedom. Here my race has been afforded [the] opportunity to advance from a people 80 percent illiterate to a people 80 percent literate; from abject poverty to the ownership and operation of a million farms and 750,000 homes; from total disfranchisement to participation in government; from the status of chattels to recognized contributors to the American culture.

As we have been extended a *measure* of democracy, we have brought to the nation rich gifts. We have helped to build America with our labor, strengthened it with our faith and enriched it with our song. We have given you Paul Lawrence Dunbar, Booker T. Washington, Marian Anderson and George Washington Carver. But even these are only the first fruits of a rich harvest, which will be reaped when new and wider fields are opened to us.

The democratic doors of equal opportunity have not been opened wide to Negroes. In the Deep South, Negro youth is offered only one-fifteenth of the educational opportunity of the average American child. The great masses of Negro workers are depressed and unprotected in the lowest levels of agriculture and domestic service, while the black workers in industry are barred from certain unions and generally assigned to the more laborious and poorly paid work. Their housing and living conditions are sordid and unhealthy. They live too often in terror of the lynch mob; are deprived too often of the Constitutional right of suffrage; and are humiliated too often by the denial of civil liberties. We do not believe that justice and common decency will allow these conditions to continue.

Our faith in visions of fundamental change as mutual respect and understanding between our races come in the path of spiritual awakening. Certainly there have been times when we may have delayed this mutual understanding by being slow to assume a fuller share of our national responsibility because of the denial of full equality. And yet, we have always been loyal when the ideals of American democracy have been attacked. We have given our *blood* in its defense—from Crispus Attucks on Boston Commons to the battlefields of France. We have fought for the democratic principles of equality under the law, equality of opportunity, equality at the ballot box, for the guarantees of life, liberty and the pursuit of happiness. We have fought to preserve one nation, conceived in liberty and dedicated to the proposition that *all* men are created equal. Yes, we have fought for America with all her imperfections, not so much for what she is, but for what we *know* she can be.

Perhaps the greatest battle is before us, the fight for a new America: fearless, free, united, morally re-armed, in which 12 million Negroes, shoulder to shoulder with their fellow Americans, will strive that this nation under God will have a new birth of freedom, and that government of the people, for the people and by the people shall not perish from the earth. This dream, this idea, this aspiration, *this* is what American democracy means to me. [Applause.]

Martin Luther King, Jr.

(1929–1968)

I HAVE A DREAM
August 28, 1963

Perhaps the most important civil rights leader in American history, Martin Luther King, Jr., preached a message of nonviolence and passive resistance as the means for achieving social change. The son of a Baptist preacher, King went on to follow in his father's footsteps, becoming minister of the Dexter Avenue Baptist Church in Montgomery, Alabama. He devoted his life to the advancement of the principles set forth in the following speech, which he delivered from the steps of the Lincoln Memorial during the outdoor gathering of the 1963 Civil Rights March, in Washington, D.C. In 1964 King was awarded the Nobel Peace Prize; he was assassinated in 1968.

I AM HAPPY to join with you today in what will go down in history as the greatest demonstration for freedom in the history of our nation.

Five score years ago, a great American, in whose symbolic shadow we stand, signed the Emancipation Proclamation. This momentous decree came as a great beacon light of hope to millions of Negro slaves who had been seared in the flames of withering injustice. It came as a joyous daybreak to end the long night of captivity.

But one hundred years later, we must face the tragic fact that the Negro still is not free. One hundred years later, the life of the Negro is still sadly crippled by the manacles of segregation and the chains of discrimination. One hundred years later, the Negro lives on a lonely island of poverty in the midst of a vast ocean of material prosperity. One hundred years later, the Negro is still languishing in the corners of American society and finds himself an exile in his own land. And so we've come here today to dramatize an appalling condition.

In a sense we have come to our nation's Capital to cash a check. When the architects of our republic wrote the magnificent words of the Constitution and the Declaration of Independence, they were signing a promissory note to which every American was to fall heir. This note was a promise that all men would be guaranteed the unalienable rights of life, liberty, and the pursuit of happiness.

It is obvious today that America has defaulted on this promissory note insofar as her citizens of color are concerned. Instead of honoring this sacred obligation, America has given the Negro people a bad check; a check which has come back marked "insufficient funds." But we refuse to believe that the bank of justice is bankrupt. We refuse to believe that there are insufficient funds in the great vaults of opportunity of this nation. So we have come to cash this check—a check that will give us upon demand the riches of freedom and the security of justice. We have also come to this hallowed spot to remind America of the fierce urgency of *now*. This is no time to engage in the luxury of cooling off or to take the tranquilizing drug of gradualism. *Now* is the time to make real the promises of Democracy. *Now* is the time to rise from the dark and desolate valley of segregation to the sunlit path of racial justice. *Now* is the time to open the doors of opportunity to all of God's children. *Now* is the time to lift our nation from the quicksands of racial injustice to the solid rock of brotherhood.

It would be fatal for the nation to overlook the urgency of the moment and to underestimate the determination of the Negro. This sweltering summer of the Negro's legitimate discontent will not pass until there is an invigorating autumn of freedom and equality. Nineteen sixty-three is not an end, but a beginning. Those who hope that the Negro needed to blow off steam and will now be content will have a rude awakening if the Nation returns to business as usual. There will be neither rest nor tranquility in America until the Negro is granted his citizenship rights. The whirlwinds of revolt will continue to shake the foundations of our Nation until the bright day of justice emerges.

But there is something that I must say to my people who stand on the warm threshold which leads into the palace of justice. In the process of gaining our rightful place we must not be guilty of wrongful deeds. Let us not seek to satisfy our thirst for freedom by drinking from the cup of bitterness and hatred. We must forever conduct our struggle on the high plane of dignity and discipline. We must not allow our creative protest to degenerate into physical violence. Again and again we must rise to the majestic heights of meeting physical force with soul force. The marvelous new militancy which has engulfed the Negro community must not lead us to a distrust of all white people, for many of our white brothers, as evidenced by their presence here today, have come to realize that their destiny is tied up with our destiny. And they have come to realize that their freedom is inextricably bound to our freedom. We cannot walk alone.

And as we walk, we must make the pledge that we shall march ahead. We cannot turn back. There are those who are asking the devotees of civil rights, "When will you be satisfied?" We can never be satisfied as long as the Negro is the victim of the unspeakable horrors of police brutality. We can never be satisfied as long as our bodies, heavy with the fatigue of travel, cannot gain lodging in the motels of the highways and the hotels of the cities. We cannot be satisfied as long as the Negro's basic mobility is from a smaller ghetto to a larger one. We can never be satisfied as long as a Negro in Mississippi cannot vote and a Negro in New York believes he has nothing for which to vote. No, no, we are not satisfied, and we will not be satisfied until justice rolls down like waters and righteousness like a mighty stream.

I am not unmindful that some of you have come here out of great trials and tribulations. Some of you have come fresh from narrow jail cells. Some of you have come from areas where your quest for freedom left you battered by the storms of persecution and staggered by the winds of police brutality. You have been the veterans of creative suffering. Continue to work with the faith that unearned suffering is redemptive.

Go back to Mississippi, go back to Alabama, go back to South Carolina, go back to Georgia, go back to Louisiana, go back to the slums and ghettos of our modern cities, knowing that somehow this situation can and will be changed. Let us not wallow in the valley of despair.

I say to you today, my friends, that in spite of the difficulties and frustrations of the moment, I still have a dream. It is a dream deeply rooted in the American dream.

I have a dream that one day this nation will rise up and live out the true meaning of its creed: "We hold these truths to be self-evident; that all men are created equal."

I have a dream that one day on the red hills of Georgia the sons of former slaves and the sons of former slaveowners will be able to sit down together at the table of brotherhood.

I have a dream that one day even the state of Mississippi, a desert state sweltering with the heat of injustice and oppression, will be transformed into an oasis of freedom and justice.

I have a dream that my four little children will one day live in a nation where they will not be judged by the color of their skin but by the content of their character.

I have a dream today.

I have a dream that one day the state of Alabama, whose governor's lips are presently dripping with the words of interposition and nullification, will be transformed into a situation where little black boys and black girls will be able to join hands with little white boys and white girls and walk together as sisters and brothers.

I have a dream today.

I have a dream that one day every valley shall be exalted, every hill and mountain shall be made low, the rough places will be made plains, and the crooked places will be made straight; and the glory of the Lord shall be revealed, and all flesh shall see it together.

This is our hope. This is the faith with which I return to the South. With this faith we will be able to hew out of the mountain of despair a stone of hope. With this faith we will be able to transform the jangling discords of our nation into a beautiful symphony of brotherhood. With this faith we will be able to work together, to pray together, to struggle together, to go to jail together, to stand up for freedom together, knowing that we will be free one day.

And this will be the day when all of God's children will be able to sing with new meaning:"My country 'tis of thee, sweet land of liberty, of thee I sing. Land where my fathers died, land of the pilgrim's pride, from every mountainside, let freedom ring."

And if America is to be a great nation, this must become true. So let freedom ring from the prodigious hilltops of New Hampshire. Let freedom ring from the mighty mountains of New York. Let freedom ring from the heightening Alleghenies of Pennsylvania!

Let freedom ring from the snowcapped Rockies of Colorado!

Let freedom ring from the curvaceous peaks of California!

But not only that; let freedom ring from Stone Mountain of Georgia!

Let freedom ring from Lookout Mountain of Tennessee.

Let freedom ring from every hill and mole hill of Mississippi. From every mountainside, let freedom ring.

When we let freedom ring, when we let it ring from every village and every hamlet, from every state and every city, we will be able to speed up that day when all of God's children, black men and white men, Jews and Gentiles, Protestants and Catholics, will be able to join hands and sing in the words of the old Negro spiritual, "Free at last! free at last! thank God almighty, we are free at last!"

Malcolm X

(1925–1965)

THE BALLOT OR THE BULLET
April 3, 1964

Born in Omaha, Nebraska, and raised in Lansing, Michigan, Malcolm X was the product of a tumultuous childhood: his house was burned down by the Ku Klux Klan, his father murdered, and his mother placed in a mental institution. After spending years in detention homes, Malcolm was converted to the Nation of Islam while in prison and appointed to be a speaker for the Nation of Islam upon his release. In the years that followed, Malcolm X made a name for himself as an influential advocate of militant black nationalism, eventually parting ways with the Nation of Islam. The following speech was delivered at the Cory Methodist Church in Cleveland, Ohio, less than a year before Malcolm's assassination.

MR. MODERATOR, Brother Lomax, brothers and sisters, friends and enemies: I just can't believe everyone in here is a friend, and I don't want to leave anybody out. The question tonight, as I understand it, is "The Negro Revolt, and Where Do We Go From Here?" or "What Next?" In my little humble way of understanding it, it points toward either the ballot or the bullet.

Before we try and explain what is meant by the ballot or the bullet, I would like to clarify something concerning myself. I'm still a Muslim; my religion is still Islam. That's my personal belief. Just as Adam Clayton Powell is a Christian minister who heads the Abyssinian Baptist Church in New York, but at the same time takes part in the political struggles to try and bring about rights to the black people in this country; and Dr. Martin Luther King is a Christian minister down in Atlanta, Georgia, who heads another organization fighting for the civil rights of black people in this country; and Reverend Galamison, I guess you've heard of him, is another Christian minister in New York who has been deeply involved in the school boycotts to eliminate segregated education; well, I myself am a minister, not a Christian minister, but a Muslim minister; and I believe in action on all fronts by whatever means necessary.

Although I'm still a Muslim, I'm not here tonight to discuss my religion. I'm not here to try and change your religion. I'm not here to argue or discuss anything that we differ about, because it's time for us to submerge our differences and realize that it is best for us to first see that we have the same problem, a common problem, a problem that will make you catch hell whether you're a Baptist, or a Methodist, or a Muslim, or a nationalist. Whether you're educated or illiterate, whether you live on the boulevard or in the alley, you're going to catch hell just like I am. We're all in the same boat and we all are going to catch the same hell from the same man. He just happens to be a white man. All of us have suffered here, in this country, political oppression at the hands of the white man, economic exploitation at the hands of the white man, and social degradation at the hands of the white man.

Now in speaking like this, it doesn't mean that we're anti-white, but it does mean we're anti-exploitation, we're anti-degradation, we're anti-oppression. And if the white man doesn't want us to be anti-him, let him stop oppressing and exploiting and degrading us. Whether we are Christians or Muslims or nationalists or agnostics or atheists, we must first learn to forget our differences. If we have differences, let us differ in the closet; when we come out in front, let us not have anything to argue about until we get finished arguing with the man. If the late President Kennedy could get together with Khrushchev and exchange some wheat, we certainly have more in common with each other than Kennedy and Khrushchev had with each other.

If we don't do something real soon, I think you'll have to agree that we're going to be forced either to use the ballot or the bullet. It's one or the other in 1964. It isn't that time is running out—time has run out!

Nineteen-sixty-four threatens to be the most explosive year America has ever witnessed. The most explosive year. Why? It's also a political year. It's the year when all of the white politicians will be back in the so-called Negro community jiving you and me for some votes. The year when all of the white political crooks will be right back in your and my community with their false promises, building up our hopes for a letdown, with their trickery and their treachery, with their false promises which they don't intend to keep. As they nourish these dissatisfactions, it can only lead to one thing, an explosion; and now we have the type of black man on the scene in America today—I'm sorry, Brother Lomax—who just doesn't intend to turn the other cheek any longer.

Don't let anybody tell you anything about the odds are against you. If they draft you, they send you to Korea and make you face 800 million Chinese. If you can be brave over there, you can be brave right here. These odds aren't as great as those odds. And if you fight here, you will at least know what you're fighting for.

I'm not a politician, not even a student of politics; in fact, I'm not a student of much of anything. I'm not a Democrat. I'm not a Republican, and I don't even consider myself an American. If you and I were Americans, there'd be no problem. Those Honkies that just got off the boat, they're already Americans; Polacks are already Americans; the Italian refugees are already Americans. Everything that came out of Europe, every blue-eyed thing, is already an American. And as long as you and I have been over here, we aren't Americans yet.

Well, I am one who doesn't believe in deluding myself. I'm not going to sit at your table and watch you eat, with nothing on my plate, and call myself a diner. Sitting at the table doesn't make you a diner, unless you eat some of what's on that plate. Being here in America doesn't make you an American. Being born here in America doesn't make you an American. Why, if birth made you American, you wouldn't need any legislation; you wouldn't need any amendments to the Constitution; you wouldn't be faced with civil-rights filibustering in Washington, D.C., right now. They don't have to pass civil-rights legislation to make a Polack an American.

No, I'm not an American. I'm one of the 22 million black people who are the victims of Americanism. One of the 22 million black people who are the victims of democracy, nothing but disguised hypocrisy. So, I'm not standing here speaking to you as an American, or a patriot, or a flag-saluter, or a flag-waver—no, not I. I'm speaking as a victim of this American system. And I see America through the eyes of the victim. I don't see any American dream; I see an American nightmare.

These 22 million victims are waking up. Their eyes are coming open. They're beginning to see what they used to only look at. They're becoming politically mature. They are realizing that there are new political trends from coast to coast. As they see these new political trends, it's possible for them to see that every time there's an election the races are so close that they have to have a recount. They had to recount in Massachusetts to see who was going to be governor, it was so close. It was the same way in Rhode Island, in Minnesota, and in many other parts of the country. And the same with Kennedy and Nixon when they ran for president. It was so close they had to count all over again. Well, what does this mean? It means that when white people are evenly divided, and black people have a bloc of votes of their own, it is left up to them to determine who's going to sit in the White House and who's going to be in the dog house.

It was the black man's vote that put the present administration in Washington, D.C. Your vote, your dumb vote, your ignorant vote, your wasted vote put in an administration in Washington, D.C., that has seen fit to pass every kind of legislation imaginable, saving you until last, then filibustering on top of that. And your and my leaders have the audacity to run around clapping their hands and talk about how much progress we're making. And what a good president we have. If he wasn't good in Texas, he sure can't be good in Washington, D.C. Because Texas is a lynch state. It is in the same breath as Mississippi, no different; only they lynch you in Texas with a Texas accent and lynch you in Mississippi with a Mississippi accent. And these Negro leaders have the audacity to go and have some coffee in the White House with a Texan, a Southern cracker—that's all he is—and then come out and tell you and me that he's going to be better for us because, since he's from the South, he knows how to deal with the Southerners. What kind of logic is that? Let Eastland be president, he's from the South too. He should be better able to deal with them than Johnson.

In this present administration they have in the House of Representatives 257 Democrats to only 177 Republicans. They control two-thirds of the House vote. Why can't they pass something that will help you and me? In the Senate, there are 67 senators who are of the Democratic Party. Only 33 of them are Republicans. Why, the Democrats have got the government sewed up, and you're the one who sewed it up for them. And what have they given you for it? Four years in office, and just now getting around to some civil-rights legislation. Just now, after everything else is gone, out of the way, they're going to sit down now and play with you all summer long—the same old giant con game that they call filibuster. All those are in cahoots together. Don't you ever think they're not in cahoots together, for the man that is heading the civil-rights filibuster is a man from Georgia named Richard Russell. When Johnson became president, the first man he asked for when he got back to Washington, D.C., was "Dicky"—that's how tight they are. That's his boy, that's his pal, that's his buddy. But they're playing that old con game. One of them makes believe he's for you, and he's got it fixed where the other one is so tight against you, he never has to keep his promise.

So it's time in 1964 to wake up. And when you see them coming up with that kind of conspiracy, let them know your eyes are open. And let them know you—something else that's wide open too. It's got to be the ballot or the bullet. The ballot or the bullet. If you're afraid to use an expression like that, you should get on out of the country; you should get back in the cotton patch; you should get back in the alley. They get all the Negro vote, and after they get it, the Negro gets nothing in return. All they did when they got to Washington was give a few big Negroes big jobs. Those big Negroes didn't need big jobs, they already had jobs. That's camouflage, that's trickery, that's treachery, window-dressing. I'm not trying to knock out the Democrats for the Republicans. We'll get to them in a minute. But it is true; you put the Democrats first and the Democrats put you last.

Look at it the way it is. What alibis do they use, since they control Congress and the Senate? What alibi do they use when you and I ask, "Well, when are you going to keep your promise?" They blame the Dixiecrats. What is a Dixiecrat? A Democrat. A Dixiecrat is nothing but a Democrat in disguise. The titular head of the Democrats is also the head of the Dixiecrats, because the Dixiecrats are a part of the Democratic Party. The Democrats have never kicked the Dixiecrats out of the party. The Dixiecrats bolted themselves once, but the Democrats didn't put them out. Imagine, these lowdown Southern segregationists put the Northern Democrats down. But the Northern Democrats have never put the Dixiecrats down. No, look at that thing the way it is. They have got a con game going on, a political con game, and you and I are in the middle. It's time for you and me to wake up and start looking at it like it is, and trying to understand it like it is; and then we can deal with it like it is.

The Dixiecrats in Washington, D.C., control the key committees that run the government. The only reason the Dixiecrats control these committees is because they have seniority. The only reason they have seniority is because they come from states where Negroes can't vote. This is not even a government that's based on democracy. It is not a government that is made up of representatives of the people. Half of the people in the South can't even vote. Eastland is not even supposed to be in Washington. Half of the senators and congressmen who occupy these key positions in Washington, D.C., are there illegally, are there unconstitutionally.

I was in Washington, D.C., a week ago Thursday, when they were debating whether or not they should let the bill come onto the floor. And in the back of the room where the Senate meets, there's a huge map of the United States, and on that map it shows the location of Negroes throughout the country. And it shows that the Southern section of the country, the states that are most heavily concentrated with Negroes, are the ones that have senators and congressmen standing up filibustering and doing all other kinds of trickery to keep the Negro from being able to vote. This is pitiful. But it's not pitiful for us any longer; it's actually pitiful for the white man, because soon now, as the Negro awakens a little more and sees the vise that he's in, sees the bag that he's in, sees the real game that he's in, then the Negro's going to develop a new tactic.

These senators and congressmen actually violate the constitutional amendments that guarantee the people of that particular state or county the right to vote. And the Constitution itself has within it the machinery to expel any representative from a state where the voting rights of the people are violated. You don't even need new legislation. Any person in Congress right now, who is there from a state or a district where the voting rights of the people are violated, that particular person should be expelled from Congress. And when you expel him, you've removed one of the obstacles in the path of any real meaningful legislation in this country. In fact, when you expel them, you don't need new legislation, because they will be replaced by black representatives from counties and districts where the black man is in the majority, not in the minority.

If the black man in these Southern states had his full voting rights, the key Dixiecrats in Washington, D.C., which means the key Democrats in Washington, D.C., would lose their seats. The Democratic Party itself would lose its power. It would cease to be powerful as a party. When you see the amount of power that would be lost by the Democratic Party if it were to lose the Dixiecrat wing, or branch, or element, you can see where it's against the interests of the Democrats to give voting rights to Negroes in states where the Democrats have been in complete power and authority ever since the Civil War. You just can't belong to that Party without analyzing it.

I say again, I'm not anti-Democrat, I'm not anti-Republican, I'm not anti-anything. I'm just questioning their sincerity, and some of the strategy that they've been using on our people by promising them promises that they don't intend to keep. When you keep the Democrats in power, you're keeping the Dixiecrats in power. I doubt that my good Brother Lomax will deny that. A vote for a Democrat is a vote for a Dixiecrat. That's why, in 1964, it's time now for you and me to become more politically mature and realize what the ballot is for; what we're supposed to get when we cast a ballot; and that if we don't cast a ballot, it's going to end up in a situation where we're going to have to cast a bullet. It's either a ballot or a bullet.

In the North, they do it a different way. They have a system that's known as gerrymandering, whatever that means. It means when Negroes become too heavily concentrated in a certain area, and begin to gain too much political power, the white man comes along and changes the district lines. You may say, "Why do you keep saying white man?" Because it's the white man who does it. I haven't ever seen any Negro changing any lines. They don't let him get near the line. It's the white man who does this. And usually, it's the white man who grins at you the most, and pats you on the back, and is supposed to be your friend. He may be friendly, but he's not your friend.

So, what I'm trying to impress upon you, in essence, is this: You and I in America are faced not with a segregationist conspiracy, we're faced with a government conspiracy. Everyone who's filibustering is a senator—that's the government. Everyone who's finagling in Washington, D.C., is a congressman—that's the government. You don't have anybody putting blocks in your path but people who are a part of the government. The same government that you go abroad to fight for and die for is the government that is in a conspiracy to deprive you of your voting rights, deprive you of your economic opportunities, deprive you of decent housing, deprive you of decent education. You don't need to go to the employer alone, it is the government itself, the government of America, that is responsible for the oppression and exploitation and degradation of black people in this country. And you should drop it in their lap. This government has failed the Negro. This so-called democracy has failed the Negro. And all these white liberals have definitely failed the Negro.

So, where do we go from here? First, we need some friends. We need some new allies. The entire civil-rights struggle needs a new interpretation, a broader interpretation. We need to look at this civil-rights thing from another angle—from the inside as well as from the outside. To those of us whose philosophy is black nationalism, the only way you can get involved in the civil-rights struggle is give it a new interpretation. That old interpretation excluded us. It kept us out. So, we're giving a new interpretation to the civil-rights struggle, an interpretation that will enable us to come into it, take part in it. And these handkerchief-heads who have been dillydallying and pussyfooting and compromising—we don't intend to let them pussyfoot and dillydally and compromise any longer.

How can you thank a man for giving you what's already yours? How then can you thank him for giving you only part of what's already yours? You haven't even made progress, if what's being given to you, you should have had already. That's not progress. And I love my Brother Lomax, the way he pointed out we're right back where we were in 1954. We're not even as far up as we were in 1954. We're behind where we were in 1954. There's more segregation now than there was in 1954. There's more racial animosity, more racial hatred, more racial violence today in 1964, than there was in 1954. Where is the progress?

And now you're facing a situation where the young Negro's coming up. They don't want to hear that "turn the-other-cheek" stuff, no. In Jacksonville, those were teenagers, they were throwing Molotov cocktails. Negroes have never done that before. But it shows you there's a new deal coming in. There's new thinking coming in. There's new strategy coming in. It'll be Molotov cocktails this month, hand grenades next month, and something else next month. It'll be ballots, or it'll be bullets. It'll be liberty, or it will be death. The only difference about this kind of death—it'll be reciprocal. You know what is meant by "reciprocal"? That's one of Brother Lomax's words. I stole it from him. I don't usually deal with those big words because I don't usually deal with big people. I deal with small people. I find you can get a whole lot of small people and whip hell out of a whole lot of big people. They haven't got anything to lose, and they've got every thing to gain. And they'll let you know in a minute: "It takes two to tango; when I go, you go."

The black nationalists, those whose philosophy is black nationalism, in bringing about this new interpretation of the entire meaning of civil rights, look upon it as meaning, as Brother Lomax has pointed out, equality of opportunity. Well, we're justified in seeking civil rights, if it means equality of opportunity, because all we're doing there is trying to collect for our investment. Our mothers and fathers invested sweat and blood. Three hundred and ten years we worked in this country without a dime in return—I mean without a dime in return. You let the white man walk around here talking about how rich this country is, but you never stop to think how it got rich so quick. It got rich because you made it rich.

You take the people who are in this audience right now. They're poor. We're all poor as individuals. Our weekly salary individually amounts to hardly anything. But if you take the salary of everyone in here collectively, it'll fill up a whole lot of baskets. It's a lot of wealth. If you can collect the wages of just these people right here for a year, you'll be rich—richer than rich. When you look at it like that, think how rich Uncle Sam had to become, not with this handful, but millions of black people. Your and my mother and father, who didn't work an eight-hour shift, but worked from "can't see" in the morning until "can't see" at night, and worked for nothing, making the white man rich, making Uncle Sam rich. This is our investment. This is our contribution, our blood.

Not only did we give of our free labor, we gave of our blood. Every time he had a call to arms, we were the first ones in uniform. We died on every battlefield the white man had. We have made a greater sacrifice than anybody who's standing up in America today. We have made a greater contribution and have collected less. Civil rights, for those of us whose philosophy is black nationalism, means: "Give it to us now. Don't wait for next year. Give it to us yesterday, and that's not fast enough."

I might stop right here to point out one thing. Whenever you're going after something that belongs to you, anyone who's depriving you of the right to have it is a criminal. Understand that. Whenever you are going after something that is yours, you are within your legal rights to lay claim to it. And anyone who puts forth any effort to deprive you of that which is yours, is breaking the law, is a criminal. And this was pointed out by the Supreme Court decision. It outlawed segregation.

Which means segregation is against the law. Which means a segregationist is breaking the law. A segregationist is a criminal. You can't label him as anything other than that. And when you demonstrate against segregation, the law is on your side. The Supreme Court is on your side.

Now, who is it that opposes you in carrying out the law? The police department itself. With police dogs and clubs. Whenever you demonstrate against segregation, whether it is segregated education, segregated housing, or anything else, the law is on your side, and anyone who stands in the way is not the law any longer. They are breaking the law; they are not representatives of the law. Any time you demonstrate against segregation and a man has the audacity to put a police dog on you, kill that dog, kill him, I'm telling you, kill that dog. I say it, if they put me in jail tomorrow, kill that dog. Then you'll put a stop to it. Now, if these white people in here don't want to see that kind of action, get down and tell the mayor to tell the police department to pull the dogs in. That's all you have to do. If you don't do it, someone else will.

If you don't take this kind of stand, your little children will grow up and look at you and think "shame." If you don't take an uncompromising stand, I don't mean go out and get violent; but at the same time you should never be nonviolent unless you run into some nonviolence. I'm nonviolent with those who are nonviolent with me. But when you drop that violence on me, then you've made me go insane, and I'm not responsible for what I do. And that's the way every Negro should get. Any time you know you're within the law, within your legal rights, within your moral rights, in accord with justice, then die for what you believe in. But don't die alone. Let your dying be reciprocal. This is what is meant by equality. What's good for the goose is good for the gander.

When we begin to get in this area, we need new friends, we need new allies. We need to expand the civil-rights struggle to a higher level—to the level of human rights. Whenever you are in a civil-rights struggle, whether you know it or not, you are confining yourself to the jurisdiction of Uncle Sam. No one from the outside world can speak out in your behalf as long as your struggle is a civil-rights struggle. Civil rights comes within the domestic affairs of this country. All of our African brothers and our Asian brothers and our Latin-American brothers cannot open their mouths and interfere in the domestic affairs of the United States. And as long as it's civil rights, this comes under the jurisdiction of Uncle Sam.

But the United Nations has what's known as the charter of human rights; it has a committee that deals in human rights. You may wonder why all of the atrocities that have been committed in Africa and in Hungary and in Asia, and in Latin America are brought before the UN, and the Negro problem is never brought before the UN. This is part of the conspiracy. This old, tricky blue-eyed liberal who is supposed to be your and my friend, supposed to be in our corner, supposed to be subsidizing our struggle, and supposed to be acting in the capacity of an adviser, never tells you anything about human rights. They keep you wrapped up in civil rights. And you spend so much time barking up the civil-rights tree, you don't even know there's a human-rights tree on the same floor.

When you expand the civil-rights struggle to the level of human rights, you can then take the case of the black man in this country before the nations in the UN. You can take it before the General Assembly. You can take Uncle Sam before a world court. But the only level you can do it on is the level of human rights. Civil rights keeps you under his restrictions, under his jurisdiction. Civil rights keeps you in his pocket. Civil rights means you're asking Uncle Sam to treat you right. Human rights are something you were born with. Human rights are your God-given rights. Human rights are the rights that are recognized by all nations of this earth. And any time any one violates your human rights, you can take them to the world court.

Uncle Sam's hands are dripping with blood, dripping with the blood of the black man in this country. He's the earth's number-one hypocrite. He has the audacity—yes, he has—imagine him posing as the leader of the free world. The free world! And you over here singing "We Shall Overcome." Expand the civil-rights struggle to the level of human rights. Take it into the United Nations, where our African brothers can throw their weight on our side, where our Asian brothers can throw their weight on our side, where our Latin-American brothers can throw their weight on our side, and where 800 million Chinamen are sitting there waiting to throw their weight on our side.

Let the world know how bloody his hands are. Let the world know the hypocrisy that's practiced over here. Let it be the ballot or the bullet. Let him know that it must be the ballot or the bullet.

When you take your case to Washington, D.C., you're taking it to the criminal who's responsible; it's like running from the wolf to the fox. They're all in cahoots together. They all work political chicanery and make you look like a chump before the eyes of the world. Here you are walking around in America, getting ready to be drafted and sent abroad, like a tin soldier, and when you get over there, people ask you what are you fighting for, and you have to stick your tongue in your cheek. No, take Uncle Sam to court, take him before the world.

By ballot I only mean freedom. Don't you know—I disagree with Lomax on this issue—that the ballot is more important than the dollar? Can I prove it? Yes. Look in the UN. There are poor nations in the UN; yet those poor nations can get together with their voting power and keep the rich nations from making a move. They have one nation—one vote, everyone has an equal vote. And when those brothers from Asia, and Africa and the darker parts of this earth get together, their voting power is sufficient to hold Sam in check. Or Russia in check. Or some other section of the earth in check. So, the ballot is most important.

Right now, in this country, if you and I, 22 million African-Americans—that's what we are—Africans who are in America. You're nothing but Africans. Nothing but Africans. In fact, you'd get farther calling yourself African instead of Negro. Africans don't catch hell. You're the only one catching hell. They don't have to pass civil-rights bills for Africans. An African can go anywhere he wants right now. All you've got to do is tie your head up. That's right, go anywhere you want. Just stop being a Negro. Change your name to Hoogagagooba. That'll show you how silly the white man is. You're dealing with a silly man. A friend of mine who's very dark put a turban on his head and went into a restaurant in Atlanta before they called themselves desegregated. He went into a white restaurant, he sat down, they served him, and he said, "What would happen if a Negro came in here?" And there he's sitting, black as night, but because he had his head wrapped up the waitress looked back at him and says, "Why, there wouldn't no nigger dare come in here."

So, you're dealing with a man whose bias and prejudice are making him lose his mind, his intelligence, every day. He's frightened. He looks around and sees what's taking place on this earth, and he sees that the pendulum of time is swinging in your direction. The dark people are waking up. They're losing their fear of the white man. No place where he's fighting right now is he winning. Everywhere he's fighting, he's fighting someone your and my complexion. And they're beating him. He can't win any more. He's won his last battle. He failed to win the Korean War. He couldn't win it. He had to sign a truce. That's a loss.

Any time Uncle Sam, with all his machinery for warfare, is held to a draw by some rice eaters, he's lost the battle. He had to sign a truce. America's not supposed to sign a truce. She's supposed to be bad. But she's not bad any more. She's bad as long as she can use her hydrogen bomb, but she can't use hers for fear Russia might use hers. Russia can't use hers, for fear that Sam might use his. So, both of them are weapon-less. They can't use the weapon because each's weapon nullifies the other's. So the only place where action can take place is on the ground. And the white man can't win another war fighting on the ground. Those days are over. The black man knows it, the brown man knows it, the red man knows it, and the yellow man knows it. So they engage him in guerrilla warfare. That's not his style. You've got to have heart to be a guerrilla warrior, and he hasn't got any heart. I'm telling you now.

I just want to give you a little briefing on guerrilla warfare because, before you know it, before you know it. It takes heart to be a guerrilla warrior because you're on your own. In conventional warfare you have tanks and a whole lot of other people with you to back you up—planes over your head and all that kind of stuff. But a guerrilla is on his own. All you have is a rifle, some sneakers and a bowl of rice, and that's all you need—and a lot of heart. The Japanese on some of those islands in the Pacific, when the American soldiers landed, one Japanese sometimes could hold the whole army off. He'd just wait until the sun went down, and when the sun went down they were all equal. He would take his little blade and slip from bush to bush, and from American to American. The white soldiers couldn't cope with that. Whenever you see a white soldier that fought in the Pacific, he has the shakes, he has a nervous condition, because they scared him to death.

The same thing happened to the French up in French Indochina. People who just a few years previously were rice farmers got together and ran the heavily-mechanized French army out of Indochina. You don't need it—modern warfare today won't work. This is the day of the guerrilla. They did the same thing in Algeria. Algerians, who were nothing but Bedouins, took a rine and sneaked off to the hills, and de Gaulle and all of his highfalutin' war machinery couldn't defeat those guerrillas. Nowhere on this earth does the white man win in a guerrilla warfare. It's not his speed. Just as guerrilla warfare is prevailing in Asia and in parts of Africa and in parts of Latin America, you've got to be mighty naive, or you've got to play the black man cheap, if you don't think some day he's going to wake up and find that it's got to be the ballot or the bullet.

I would like to say, in closing, a few things concerning the Muslim Mosque, Inc., which we established recently in New York City. It's true we're Muslims and our religion is Islam, but we don't mix our religion with our politics and our economics and our social and civil activities—not any more. We keep our religion in our mosque. After our religious services are over, then as Muslims we become involved in political action, economic action and social and civic action. We become involved with anybody, any where, any time and in any manner that's designed to eliminate the evils, the political, economic and social evils that are afflicting the people of our community.

The political philosophy of black nationalism means that the black man should control the politics and the politicians in his own community; no more. The black man in the black community has to be re-educated into the science of politics so he will know what politics is supposed to bring him in return. Don't be throwing out any ballots. A ballot is like a bullet. You don't throw your ballots until you see a target, and if that target is not within your reach, keep your ballot in your pocket.

The political philosophy of black nationalism is being taught in the Christian church. It's being taught in the NAACP. It's being taught in CORE meetings. It's being taught in SNCC Student Nonviolent Coordinating Committee meetings. It's being taught in Muslim meetings. It's being taught where nothing but atheists and agnostics come together. It's being taught everywhere. Black people are fed up with the dillydallying, pussyfooting, compromising approach that we've been using toward getting our freedom. We want freedom now, but we're not going to get it saying "We Shall Overcome." We've got to fight until we overcome.

The economic philosophy of black nationalism is pure and simple. It only means that we should control the economy of our community. Why should white people be running all the stores in our community? Why should white people be running the banks of our community? Why should the economy of our community be in the hands of the white man? Why? If a black man can't move his store into a white community, you tell me why a white man should move his store into a black community. The philosophy of black nationalism involves a re-education program in the black community in regards to economics. Our people have to be made to see that any time you take your dollar out of your community and spend it in a community where you don't live, the community where you live will get poorer and poorer, and the community where you spend your money will get richer and richer.

Then you wonder why where you live is always a ghetto or a slum area. And where you and I are concerned, not only do we lose it when we spend it out of the community, but the white man has got all our stores in the community tied up; so that though we spend it in the community, at sundown the man who runs the store takes it over across town somewhere. He's got us in a vise.

So the economic philosophy of black nationalism means in every church, in every civic organization, in every fraternal order, it's time now for our people to become conscious of the importance of controlling the economy of our community. If we own the stores, if we operate the businesses, if we try and establish some industry in our own community, then we're developing to the position where we are creating employment for our own kind. Once you gain control of the economy of your own community, then you don't have to picket and boycott and beg some cracker downtown for a job in his business.

The social philosophy of black nationalism only means that we have to get together and remove the evils, the vices, alcoholism, drug addiction, and other evils that are destroying the moral fiber of our community. We our selves have to lift the level of our community, the standard of our community to a higher level, make our own society beautiful so that we will be satisfied in our own social circles and won't be running around here trying to knock our way into a social circle where we're not wanted. So I say, in spreading a gospel such as black nationalism, it is not designed to make the black man re-evaluate the white man—you know him already—but to make the black man re-evaluate himself. Don't change the white man's mind—you can't change his mind, and that whole thing about appealing to the moral conscience of America— America's conscience is bankrupt. She lost all conscience a long time ago. Uncle Sam has no conscience.

They don't know what morals are. They don't try and eliminate an evil because it's evil, or because it's illegal, or because it's immoral; they eliminate it only when it threatens their existence. So you're wasting your time appealing to the moral conscience of a bankrupt man like Uncle Sam. If he had a conscience, he'd straighten this thing out with no more pressure being put upon him. So it is not necessary to change the white man's mind. We have to change our own mind. You can't change his mind about us. We've got to change our own minds about each other. We have to see each other with new eyes. We have to see each other as brothers and sisters. We have to come together with warmth so we can develop unity and harmony that's necessary to get this problem solved ourselves. How can we do this? How can we avoid jealousy? How can we avoid the suspicion and the divisions that exist in the community? I'll tell you how.

I have watched how Billy Graham comes into a city, spreading what he calls the gospel of Christ, which is only white nationalism. That's what he is. Billy Graham is a white nationalist; I'm a black nationalist. But since it's the natural tendency for leaders to be jealous and look upon a powerful figure like Graham with suspicion and envy, how is it possible for him to come into a city and get all the cooperation of the church leaders? Don't think because they're church leaders that they don't have weaknesses that make them envious and jealous—no, everybody's got it. It's not an accident that when they want to choose a cardinal, as Pope over there in Rome, they get in a closet so you can't hear them cussing and fighting and carrying on.

Billy Graham comes in preaching the gospel of Christ. He evangelizes the gospel. He stirs everybody up, but he never tries to start a church. If he came in trying to start a church, all the churches would be against him. So, he just comes in talking about Christ and tells everybody who gets Christ to go to any church where Christ is; and in this way the church cooperates with him. So we're going to take a page from his book.

Our gospel is black nationalism. We're not trying to threaten the existence of any organization, but we're spreading the gospel of black nationalism. Anywhere there's a church that is also preaching and practicing the gospel of black nationalism, join that church. If the NAACP is preaching and practicing the gospel of black nationalism, join the NAACP. If CORE is spreading and practicing the gospel of black nationalism, join CORE. Join any organization that has a gospel that's for the uplift of the black man. And when you get into it and see them pussyfooting or compromising, pull out of it because that's not black nationalism. We'll find another one.

And in this manner, the organizations will increase in number and in quantity and in quality, and by August, it is then our intention to have a black nationalist convention which will consist of delegates from all over the country who are interested in the political, economic and social philosophy of black nationalism. After these delegates convene, we will hold a seminar; we will hold discussions; we will listen to everyone. We want to hear new ideas and new solutions and new answers. And at that time, if we see fit then to form a black nationalist party, we'll form a black nationalist party. If it's necessary to form a black nationalist army, we'll form a black nationalist army. It'll be the ballot or the bullet. It'll be liberty or it'll be death.

It's time for you and me to stop sitting in this country, letting some cracker senators, Northern crackers and Southern crackers, sit there in Washington, D.C., and come to a conclusion in their mind that you and I are supposed to have civil rights. There's no white man going to tell me anything about my rights. Brothers and sisters, always remember, if it doesn't take senators and congressmen and presidential proclamations to give freedom to the white man, it is not necessary for legislation or proclamation or Supreme Court decisions to give freedom to the black man. You let that white man know, if this is a country of freedom, let it be a country of freedom; and if it's not a country of freedom, change it.

We will work with anybody, anywhere, at any time, who is genuinely interested in tackling the problem head-on, nonviolently as long as the enemy is nonviolent, but violent when the enemy gets violent. We'll work with you on the voter-registration drive, we'll work with you on rent strikes, we'll work with you on school boycotts; I don't believe in any kind of integration; I'm not even worried about it, because I know you're not going to get it anyway; you're not going to get it because you're afraid to die; you've got to be ready to die if you try and force yourself on the white man, because he'll get just as violent as those crackers in Mississippi, right here in Cleveland. But we will still work with you on the school boycotts because we're against a segregated school system. A segregated school system produces children who, when they graduate, graduate with crippled minds. But this does not mean that a school is segregated because it's all black. A segregated school means a school that is controlled by people who have no real interest in it whatsoever.

Let me explain what I mean. A segregated district or community is a community in which people live, but outsiders control the politics and the economy of that community. They never refer to the white section as a segregated community. It's the all-Negro section that's a segregated community. Why? The white man controls his own school, his own bank, his own economy, his own politics, his own everything, his own community; but he also controls yours. When you're under someone else's control, you're segregated. They'll always give you the lowest or the worst that there is to offer, but it doesn't mean you're segregated just because you have your own. You've got to control your own. Just like the white man has control of his, you need to control yours.

You know the best way to get rid of segregation? The white man is more afraid of separation than he is of integration. Segregation means that he puts you away from him, but not far enough for you to be out of his jurisdiction; separation means you're gone. And the white man will integrate faster than he'll let you separate. So we will work with you against the segregated school system because it's criminal, because it is absolutely destructive, in every way imaginable, to the minds of the children who have to be exposed to that type of crippling education.

Last but not least, I must say this concerning the great controversy over rifles and shotguns. The only thing that I've ever said is that in areas where the government has proven itself either unwilling or unable to defend the lives and the property of Negroes, it's time for Negroes to defend themselves. Article number two of the constitutional amendments provides you and me the right to own a rifle or a shotgun. It is constitutionally legal to own a shotgun or a rifle. This doesn't mean you're going to get a rifle and form battalions and go out looking for white folks, although you'd be within your rights—I mean, you'd be justified; but that would be illegal and we don't do anything illegal. If the white man doesn't want the black man buying rifles and shotguns, then let the government do its job.

That's all. And don't let the white man come to you and ask you what you think about what Malcolm says—why, you old Uncle Tom. He would never ask you if he thought you were going to say, "Amen!" No, he is making a Tom out of you. So, this doesn't mean forming rifle clubs and going out looking for people, but it is time, in 1964, if you are a man, to let that man know.

If he's not going to do his job in running the government and providing you and me with the protection that our taxes are supposed to be for, since he spends all those billions for his defense budget, he certainly can't begrudge you and me spending $12 or $15 for a single-shot, or double-action. I hope you understand. Don't go out shooting people, but any time—brothers and sisters, and especially the men in this audience; some of you wearing Congressional Medals of Honor, with shoulders this wide, chests this big, muscles that big—any time you and I sit around and read where they bomb a church and murder in cold blood, not some grownups, but four little girls while they were praying to the same God the white man taught them to pray to, and you and I see the government go down and can't find who did it.

Why, this man—he can find Eichmann hiding down in Argentina somewhere. Let two or three American soldiers, who are minding somebody else's business way over in South Vietnam, get killed, and he'll send battleships, sticking his nose in their business. He wanted to send troops down to Cuba and make them have what he calls free elections—this old cracker who doesn't have free elections in his own country.

No, if you never see me another time in your life, if I die in the morning, I'll die saying one thing: the ballot or the bullet, the ballot or the bullet.

If a Negro in 1964 has to sit around and wait for some cracker senator to filibuster when it comes to the rights of black people, why, you and I should hang our heads in shame. You talk about a march on Washington in 1963, you haven't seen anything. There's some more going down in '64.

And this time they're not going like they went last year. They're not going singing "We Shall Overcome." They're not going with white friends. They're not going with placards already painted for them. They're not going with round-trip tickets. They're going with one-way tickets. And if they don't want that non-nonviolent army going down there, tell them to bring the filibuster to a halt.

The black nationalists aren't going to wait. Lyndon B. Johnson is the head of the Democratic Party. If he's for civil rights, let him go into the Senate next week and declare himself. Let him go in there right now and declare himself. Let him go in there and denounce the Southern branch of his party. Let him go in there right now and take a moral stand—right now, not later. Tell him, don't wait until election time. If he waits too long, brothers and sisters, he will be responsible for letting a condition develop in this country which will create a climate that will bring seeds up out of the ground with vegetation on the end of them looking like something these people never dreamed of. In 1964, it's the ballot or the bullet.

Thank you.

Shirley Chisholm

(1924–2005)

THE BLACK WOMAN IN CONTEMPORARY AMERICA

June 17, 1974

A native of Brooklyn, New York, Shirley Chisholm received her baccalaureate degree from Brooklyn College and her master's degree from Columbia University. In 1968, Chisholm defeated James Farmer in the race to represent New York's Twelfth Congressional District in the U.S. House of Representatives, becoming the first African-American woman elected to the U.S. Congress. Chisholm gave this speech at a conference on black women in America at the University of Missouri, Kansas City.

LADIES AND GENTLEMEN, and brothers and sisters all—I'm very glad to be here this evening. I'm very glad that I've had the opportunity to be the first lecturer with respect to the topic of the black woman in contemporary America. This has become a most talked-about topic and has caused a great deal of provocation and misunderstandings and misinterpretations. And I come to you this evening to speak on this topic not as any scholar, not as any academician, but as a person that has been out here for the past twenty years, trying to make my way as a black and a woman, and meeting all *kinds* of obstacles. [Laughter and applause.]

The black woman's role has not been placed in its proper perspective, particularly in terms of the current economic and political upheaval in America today. Since time immemorial the black man's emasculation resulted in the need of the black woman to assert herself in order to maintain some semblance of a family unit. And as a result of this historical circumstance, the black woman has developed perseverance; the black woman has developed strength; the black woman has developed tenacity of purpose and other attributes which today quite often are being looked upon negatively. She continues to be labeled a matriarch. And this is indeed a played-upon white sociological interpretation of the black woman's role that has been developed and perpetrated by Daniel Moynihan and other sociologists. [Applause.]

Black women by virtue of the role they have played in our society have much to offer toward the liberation of their people. We know that our men are coming forward, but the black race needs the collective talents and the collective abilities of black men and black women who have vital skills to supplement each other.

It is quite perturbing to divert ourselves on the dividing issue of the alleged fighting that absorbs the energies of black men and black women. Such statements as "the black woman has to step back while her black man steps forward" and "the black woman has kept back the black man" are grossly, historically incorrect and serves as a scapegoating technique to prevent us from coming together as *human* beings—some of whom are black men and some are black women. [Applause.]

The consuming interests of this type of dialogue abets the enemy in terms of taking our eyes off the ball, so that our collective talents can never redound in a beneficial manner to our ethnic group. The black woman who is educated and has ability cannot be expected to put said talent on the shelf when she can utilize these gifts side-by-side with her man. One does not learn, nor does one assist in the struggle, by standing on the sidelines, constantly complaining and criticizing. [Applause.] One learns by participating in the situation—listening, observing and then acting.

It is quite understandable why black women in the majority are not interested in walking and picketing a cocktail lounge which historically has refused to open its doors a certain two hours a day when men who have just returned from Wall Street gather in said lounge to exchange bits of business transactions that occurred on the market. This is a middle-class white woman's issue. [Applause.] This is not a priority of minority women. Another issue that black women are not overly concerned about is the "M-S" versus the "M-R-S" label. [Clapping.] For many of us this is just the use of another label which does not basically change the fundamental inherent racial attitudes found in both men and women in this society. This is just another label, and black women are not preoccupied with any more label syndromes. [Laughter.] Black women are desperately concerned with the issue of survival in a society in which the Caucasian group has never really practiced the espousal of equalitarian principles in America.

An aspect of the women's liberation movement that will and does interest many black women is the potential liberation, is the potential nationalization of daycare centers in this country. Black women can accept and understand this agenda item in the women's movement. It is important that black women utilize their brainpower and focus on issues in any movement that will redound to the benefit of their people because we can serve as a vocal and a catalytic pressure group within the so-called humanistic movements, many of whom do not really comprehend the black man and the black woman.

An increasing number of black women are beginning to feel that it is important first to become free as women, in order to contribute more fully to the task of black liberation. Some feel that black men—like all men, or most men—have placed women in the stereotypes of domestics whose duty it is to stay in the background—cook, clean, have babies, and leave all of the glory to men. [Laughter.] Black women point to the civil rights movement as an example of a subtle type of male oppression, where with few exceptions black women have not had active roles in the forefront of the fight. Some like Coretta King, Katherine Cleaver, and Betty Shabazz have come *only* to their positions in the shadows of their husbands. Yet, because of the oppression of black women, they are strongest in the fight for liberation. They have led the struggle to fight against white male supremacy, dating from slavery times. And in view of these many facts it is not surprising that black women played a crucial role in the total fight for freedom in this nation. Ida Wells kept her newspaper free by walking the streets of Memphis, Tennessee, in the 1890s with two pistols on her hips. [Laughter.] And within recent years, this militant condition of black women, who have been stifled because of racism and sexism, has been carried on by Mary McLeod Bethune, Mary Church Terrell, Daisy Bates, and Diane Nash.

The black woman lives in a society that discriminates against her on two counts. The black woman cannot be discussed in the same context as her Caucasian counterpart because of the twin jeopardy of race and sex which operates against her, and the psychological and political consequences which attend them. Black women are crushed by cultural restraints and abused by the legitimate power structure. To date, neither the black movement nor women's liberation succinctly addresses itself to the dilemma confronting the black who is female. And as a consequence of ignoring or being unable to handle the problems facing black women, black women themselves are now becoming socially and politically active.

Undoubtedly black women are cultivating new attitudes, most of which will have political repercussions in the future. They are attempting to change their conditions. The maturation of the civil rights movement by the mid '60s enabled many black women to develop interest in the American political process. From their experiences they learned that the real sources of power lay at the root of the political system. For example, black sororities and pressure groups like the National Council of Negro

Women are adept at the methods of participatory politics—particularly in regard to voting and organizing. With the arrival of the '70s, young black women are demanding recognition like the other segments of society who also desire their humanity and their individual talents to be noticed. The tradition of the black woman and the Afro-American subculture and her current interest in the political process indicate the emergence of a new political entity.

Historically she has been discouraged from participating in politics. Thus she is trapped between the walls of the dominant white culture and her own subculture, both of which encourage deference to men. Both races of women have traditionally been limited to performing such tasks as opening envelopes, hanging up posters and giving teas. [Laughter and clapping.] And the minimal involvement of black women exists because they have been systematically excluded from the political process and they are members of the politically dysfunctional black lower class. Thus, unlike white women, who escape the psychological and sociological handicaps of racism, the black woman's political involvement has been a most marginal role.

But within the last six years, the Afro-American subculture has undergone tremendous social and political transformation and these changes have altered the nature of the black community. They are beginning to realize their capacities not only as blacks, but also as women. They are beginning to understand that their cultural well-being and their social well-being would only be affirmed in connection with the total black struggle. The dominant role black women played in the civil rights movement began to allow them to grasp the significance of political power in America. So obviously black women who helped to spearhead the civil rights movement would also now, at this juncture, join and direct the vanguard which would shape and mold a new kind of political participation.

This has been acutely felt in urban areas, which have been rocked by sporadic rebellions. Nothing better illustrates the need for black women to organize politically than their unusual proximity to the most crucial issues affecting black people today. They have struggled in a wide range of protest movements to eliminate the poverty and injustice that permeates the lives of black people. In New York City, for example, welfare mothers and mothers of schoolchildren have ably demonstrated the commitment of black women to the elimination of the problems that threaten the well-being of the black family. Black women must view the problems of cities such as New York not as urban problems, but as the components of a crisis without whose elimination our family lives will neither survive nor prosper. Deprived of a stable family environment because of poverty and racial injustice, disproportionate numbers of our people must live on minimal welfare allowances that help to perpetuate the breakdown of family life. In the face of the increasing poverty beset-ting black communities, black women have a responsibility. Black women have a duty to bequeath a legacy to their children. Black women have a duty to move from the periphery of organized political activity into its main arena.

I say this on the basis of many experiences. I travel throughout this country and I've come in contact with thousands of my black sisters in all kinds of conditions in this nation. And I've said to them over and over again: it is not a question of competition against black men or brown men or red men or white men in America. It is a question of the recog-nition that, since we have a tremendous responsibility in terms of our own families, that to the best of our ability we have to give everything that is within ourselves to give—in terms of helping to make that future a better future for our little boys and our little girls, and not leave it to anybody. [Applause.]

Francis Beal describes the black woman as a slave of a slave. Let me quote: "By reducing the black man in America to such abject oppression, the black woman had no protector and she was used—and is still being used—in some cases as the scapegoat for the evils that this horrendous system has perpetrated on black men. Her physical image has been mali-ciously maligned. She has been sexually molested and abused by the white colonizer. She has suffered the worst kind of economic exploitation, hav-ing been forced to serve as the white woman's maid and wet-nurse for white offspring, while her own children were more often starving and neglected. It is the depth of degradation to be socially manipulated, phys-ically raped and used to undermine your own household—and then to be powerless to reverse this syndrome."

However, Susan Johnson notes a bit of optimism. Because Susan, a brilliant young black woman, has said that the recent strides made by the black woman in the political process is a result of the intricacies of her personality. And that is to say that as a political animal, she functions independently of her double jeopardy. Because confronted with a matri-focal past and present, she is often accused of stealing the black male's position in any situation beyond that of housewife and mother. And if that were not enough to burden the black woman, she realizes that her political mobility then threatens the doctrine of white supremacy and male superiority so deeply embedded in the American culture.

So choosing not to be a victim of self-paralysis, the black woman has been able to function in the political spectrum. And more often than not, it is the subconsciousness of the racist mind that perceives her as less harmful than the black man and thus permits her to acquire the neces-sary leverage for political mobility. This subtle component of racism could prove to be essential to the key question of how the black woman has managed some major advances in the American political process. [Laughter and applause.] It is very interesting to note that everyone—with the exception of the black woman herself—has been interpreting the black woman. [Applause.] It is very interesting to note that the time has come that black women can and must no longer be passive, complacent recipients of whatever the definitions of the sociologists, the psychologists and the psychiatrists will give to us. [Applause.] Black women have been maligned, misunderstood, misinterpreted—who knows better than Shirley Chisholm? [Applause.]

And I stand here tonight to tell to you, my sisters, that if you have the courage of your convictions, you must stand up and be counted. I hope that the day will come in America when this business of male versus female does not become such an overriding issue, so that the talents and abilities that the almighty God have given to *people* can be utilized for the benefit of humanity.[Applause.]

One has to recognize that there are stupid white women and stupid white men, stupid black women and stupid black men, brilliant white women and brilliant white men, and brilliant black women and brilliant black men. Why do we get so hung-up in America on this question of sex? Of course, in terms of the black race, we understand the historical circumstances. We understand, also, some of the subtle maneuverings and machinations behind the scenes in order to prevent black women and black men from coming together as a race of unconquerable men and women. [Applause.]

And I just want to say to you tonight, if I say nothing else: I would never have been able to make it in America if I had paid attention to all of the doomsday-criers about me. [Applause.] And I want to say in conclusion that as you have this conference here for the next two weeks, put the cards out on the table and do not be afraid to discuss issues that perhaps you have been sweeping under the rug because of what people might say about you. [Applause.] You must remember that once we are able to face the truth, the truth shall set all of us free. [Applause.]

In conclusion, I just want to say to you, black and white, north and east, south and west, men and women: the time has come in America when we should no longer be the passive, complacent recipients of whatever the morals or the politics of a nation may decree for us in this nation. Forget traditions! Forget conventionalisms! Forget what the world will say whether you're *in* your place or *out* of your place. [Applause.] Stand up and be counted. Do *your* thing, looking only to God—whoever your God is—and to your consciences for approval. I thank you. [Applause.]

Thurgood Marshall

(1908–1993)

THE CONSTITUTION: A LIVING DOCUMENT
May 6, 1987

A graduate of Lincoln University and Howard University Law School, Thurgood Marshall distinguished himself as a lawyer for the NAACP, advancing quickly to the position of chief of the NAACP Legal Defense and Educational Fund. In the subsequent two decades, Marshall proved his worth as an advocate for the cause of civil rights by winning 29 of the 32 cases he argued before the U.S. Supreme Court. Marshall was appointed to the U.S. Court of Appeals for the Second Circuit in 1961 and was named U.S. Solicitor General in 1965. He was appointed to the U.S. Supreme Court in 1967. The following speech was delivered by Marshall at the Annual Seminar of the San Francisco Patent and Trademark Law Conference in Maui, Hawaii.

THIS YEAR marks the two hundredth anniversary of the United States Constitution. A commission has been established to coordinate the celebration. The official meetings, essay contests, and festivities have begun.

The planned commemoration will span three years, and I am told 1987 is "dedicated to the memory of the Founders and the document they drafted in Philadelphia." We are to "recall the achievements of our Founders and the knowledge and experience that inspired them, the nature of the government they established, its origins, its character, and its ends, and the rights and privileges of citizenship, as well as its attendant responsibilities."

Like many anniversary celebrations, the plan for 1987 takes particular events and holds them up as the source of all the very best that has followed. Patriotic feelings will surely swell, prompting proud proclamations of the wisdom, foresight, and sense of justice shared by the Framers and reflected in a written document now yellowed with age. This is unfortunate—not the patriotism itself, but the tendency for the celebration to oversimplify, and overlook the many other events that have been instrumental to our achievements as a nation. The focus of this celebration invites a complacent belief that the vision of those who debated and compromised in Philadelphia yielded the "more perfect Union" it is said we now enjoy.

I cannot accept this invitation, for I do not believe that the meaning of the Constitution was forever "fixed" at the Philadelphia Convention. Nor do I find the wisdom, foresight, and sense of justice exhibited by the Framers particularly profound. To the contrary, the government they devised was defective from the start, requiring several amendments, a civil war, and momentous social transformation to attain the system of constitutional government, and its respect for the individual freedoms and human rights, we hold as fundamental today. When contemporary Americans cite "The Constitution," they invoke a concept that is vastly different from what the Framers barely began to construct two centuries ago.

For a sense of the evolving nature of the Constitution we need look no further than the first three words of the document's preamble: *We the people.* When the Founding Fathers used this phrase in 1787, they did not have in mind the majority of America's citizens. *We the people* included, in the words of the Framers, "the whole Number of free Persons." On a matter so basic as the right to vote, for example, Negro slaves were excluded, although they were counted for representational purposes—at three-fifths each. Women did not gain the right to vote for over a hundred and thirty years.

These omissions were intentional. The record of the Framers' debates on the slave question is especially clear: The Southern states acceded to the demands of the New England states for giving Congress broad power to regulate commerce, in exchange for the right to continue the slave trade. The perpetuation of slavery ensured the primary source of wealth in the Southern states.

Despite this clear understanding of the role slavery would play in the new republic, use of the words "slaves" and "slavery" was carefully avoided in the original document. Political representation in the Lower House of Congress was to be based on the population of "'free Persons' in each State, plus three-fifths of all 'other Persons.'" Moral principles against slavery, for those who had them, were compromised, with no explanation of the conflicting principles for which the American Revolutionary War had ostensibly been fought: the self-evident truths "that all men are created equal, that they are endowed by their Creator with certain inalienable Rights, that among these are Life, Liberty and the pursuit of Happiness."

It was not the first such compromise. Even these ringing phrases from the Declaration of Independence are filled with irony, for an early draft of what became that Declaration assailed the King of England for suppressing legislative attempts to end the slave trade and for encouraging slave rebellions. The final draft adopted in 1776 did not contain this criticism. And so again at the Constitutional Convention eloquent objections to the institution of slavery went unheeded, and its opponents eventually consented to a document which laid a foundation for the tragic events that were to follow.

Pennsylvania's Gouverneur Morris provides an example. He opposed slavery and the counting of slaves in determining the basis for representation in Congress. At the Convention he objected "that the inhabitant of Georgia [or] South Carolina who goes to the coast of Africa, and in defiance of the most sacred laws of humanity tears away his fellow creatures from their dearest connections and damns them to the most cruel bondages, shall have more votes in a Government instituted for protection of the rights of mankind, than the Citizen of Pennsylvania or New Jersey who views with a laudable horror, so nefarious a Practice." And yet Gouverneur Morris eventually accepted the three-fifths accommodation. In fact, he wrote the final draft of the Constitution, the very document the bicentennial will commemorate.

As a result of compromise, the right of the Southern states to continue importing slaves was extended, officially, at least until 1808. We know that it actually lasted a good deal longer, as the Framers possessed no monopoly on the ability to trade moral principles for self-interest. But they nevertheless set an unfortunate example. Slaves could be imported, if the commercial interests of the North were protected. To make the compromise even more palatable, customs duties would be imposed at up to ten dollars per slave as a means of raising public revenues.

No doubt it will be said, when the unpleasant truth of the history of slavery in America is mentioned during this bicentennial year, that the Constitution was a product of its times, and embodied a compromise which, under other circumstances, would not have been made. But the effects of the Framers' compromise have remained for generations. They arose from the contradiction between guaranteeing liberty and justice to all, and denying both to Negroes.

The original intent of the phrase, *We the people,* was far too clear for any ameliorating construction. Writing for the Supreme Court in 1857, Chief Justice Taney penned the following passage in the *Dred Scott* case, on the issue whether, in the eyes of the Framers, slaves were "constituent member of the sovereignty," and were to be included among *We the people:*

We think they are not, and that they are not included, and were not intended to be included. . . . They had for more than a century before been regarded as [beings of an inferior order, and altogether unfit to associate] with the white race . . . ; and so far inferior, that they had no rights which the white man was bound to respect; and that the Negro might justly and lawfully be reduced to slavery for his benefit. . . . [A]ccordingly, a Negro of the African race was regarded . . . as an article of property, and held, and bought and sold as such. . . . [N]o one seems to have doubted the correctness of the prevailing opinion of the time.

And so, nearly seven decades after the Constitutional Convention, the Supreme Court reaffirmed the prevailing opinion of the Framers regarding the rights of Negroes in America. It took a bloody civil war before the Thirteenth Amendment could be adopted to abolish slavery, though not the consequences slavery would have for future Americans.

While the Union survived the Civil War, the Constitution did not. In its place arose a new, more promising basis for justice and equality, the Fourteenth Amendment, ensuring protection of the life, liberty, and property of *all* persons against deprivations without due process, and guaranteeing equal protection of the laws. And yet almost another century would pass before any significant recognition was obtained of the rights of Black Americans to share equally even in such basic opportunities as education, housing and employment, and to have their votes counted, and counted equally. In the meantime, Blacks joined America's military to fight its wars and invested untold hours working in its factories and on its farms, contributing to the development of this country's magnificent wealth and waiting to share in its prosperity.

What is striking is the role legal principles have played throughout America's history in determining the condition of Negroes. They were enslaved by law, emancipated by law, disenfranchised and segregated by law; and, finally, they have begun to win equality by law. Along the way, new constitutional principles have emerged to meet the challenges of a changing society. The progress has been dramatic, and it will continue.

The men who gathered in Philadelphia in 1787 could not have envisioned these changes. They could not have imagined, nor would they have accepted, that the document they were drafting would one day be construed by a Supreme Court to which had been appointed a woman and the descendent of an African slave. *We the People* are no longer enslaved, but the credit does not belong to the Framers. It belongs to those who refused to acquiesce in outdated notions of "liberty," "justice," and "equality," and who strived to better them.

And so we must be careful, when focusing on the events which took place in Philadelphia two centuries ago, that we not overlook the momentous events which followed, and thereby lose our proper sense of perspective. Otherwise, the odds are that for many Americans the bicentennial celebration will be little more than a blind pilgrimage to the shrine of the original document now stored in a vault in the National Archives. If we seek, instead, a sensitive understanding of the Constitution's inherent defects, and its promising evolution through two hundred years of history, the celebration of the "Miracle at Philadelphia" will, in my view, be a far more meaningful and humbling experience. We will see that the true miracle was not the birth of the Constitution, but its life, a life nurtured through two turbulent centuries of our own making, and a life embodying much good fortune that was not.

Thus, in this bicentennial year, we may not all participate in the festivities with flag-waving fervor. Some may more quietly commemorate the suffering, struggle, and sacrifice that have triumphed over much of what was wrong with the original document, and observe the anniversary with hopes not realized and promises not fulfilled. I plan to celebrate the bicentennial of the Constitution as a living document, including the Bill of Rights and the other amendments protecting individual freedoms and human rights.

Barack Obama

(b. 1961)

KNOX COLLEGE COMMENCEMENT ADDRESS
June 4, 2005

Born in Honolulu, Hawaii, Barack Obama graduated from Columbia University in 1983 and from Harvard Law School in 1991, where he was the first African-American president of the Harvard Law Review. Obama was elected to the Illinois State Senate in 1996; he defeated Alan Keyes in the 2004 election to become the first male African-American Democrat in the U.S. Senate since the end of the Reconstruction period. Obama offered the following address to the Knox College 2005 graduating class, in Galesburg, Illinois.

GOOD MORNING President Taylor, the Board of Trustees, faculty, parents, family, friends, and the Class of 2005. Congratulations on your graduation, and thank you for allowing me the honor to be a part of it.

Well, it's been about six months now since you sent me to Washington as your U. S. Senator. And for those of you muttering under your breath "I didn't send you anywhere," that's ok too—maybe we'll hold a little Pumphandle after the ceremony and I can change your mind for next time.

So far it's been a fascinating journey. Each time I walk into the Senate floor, I'm reminded of the history, for good and for ill, that has been made there. But there have also been a few surreal moments. For example, I remember the day before I was sworn in, when we decided to hold a press conference in our office. Now, here I am, 99th in seniority—which, I was proud wasn't dead last until I found out that the only reason we aren't 100th is because Illinois is bigger than Colorado. So I'm 99th in seniority, and the reporters are all crammed into our tiny transition office that was somewhere near the janitor's closet in the basement

143

of the Dirksen Building. It's my first day in the building, I hadn't taken one vote, I hadn't introduced one bill, I hadn't even sat down at my desk, and this very earnest reporter asks:

"Senator Obama, what's your place in history?"

I laughed out loud. Place in history? I thought he was kidding! At that point, I wasn't even sure the other Senators would save me a place at the cool lunch table.

But as I was thinking about the words to share with this class, about what's next, what's possible, and what opportunities lay ahead, I think it's not a bad question to ask yourselves:

"What will be my place in history?"

In other eras, across distant lands, this is a question that could be answered with relative ease and certainty. As a servant of Rome, you knew you would spend your life forced to build somebody else's Empire. As a peasant in 11th century China, you knew that no matter how hard you worked, the local warlord might take everything you had—and that famine might come knocking on your door any day. As a subject of King George, you knew that your freedom to worship and speak and build your own life would be ultimately limited by the throne.

And then, America happened.

A place where destiny was not a destination, but a journey to be shared and shaped and remade by people who had the gall, the temerity to believe that, against all odds, they could form "a more perfect union" on this new frontier.

And as people around the world began to hear the tale of the lowly colonists who overthrew an Empire for the sake of an idea, they came. Across the oceans and the ages, they settled in Boston and Charleston, Chicago and St. Louis, Kalamazoo and Galesburg, to try and build their own American Dream. This collective dream moved forward imperfectly—it was scarred by our treatment of native peoples, betrayed by slavery, clouded by the subjugation of women, shaken by war and depression. And yet, brick by brick, rail by rail, calloused hand by calloused hand, people kept dreaming, and building, and working, and marching, and petitioning their government, until they made America a land where the question of our place in history is not answered for us, but by us.

Have we failed at times? Absolutely. Will you occasionally fail when you embark on your own American journey? Surely. But the test is not perfection.

The true test of the American ideal is whether we are able to recognize our failings and then rise together to meet the challenges of our time. Whether we allow ourselves to be shaped by events and history, or whether we act to shape them. Whether chance of birth or circumstance decides life's big winners and losers, or whether we build a community where, at the very least, everyone has a chance to work hard, get ahead, and reach their dreams.

We have faced this choice before.

At the end of the Civil War, when farmers and their families began moving into the cities to work in the big factories that were sprouting up all across America, we had to decide: Do we do nothing and allow the captains of industry and robber barons to run roughshod over the economy and workers by competing to see who can pay the lowest wage at the worst working conditions?

Or do we try to make the system work by setting up basic rules for the market, and instituting the first public schools, and busting up monopolies, and letting workers organize into unions?

We chose to act, and we rose together.

When the irrational exuberance of the Roaring Twenties came crashing down with the stock market, we had to decide: do we follow the call of leaders who would do nothing, or the call of a leader who, perhaps because of his physical paralysis, refused to accept political paralysis?

We chose to act—regulating the market, putting people back to work, expanding bargaining rights to include health care and a secure retirement—and together we rose.

When World War II required the most massive home-front mobilization in history and we needed every single American to lend a hand, we had to decide: Do we listen to the skeptics who told us it wasn't possible to produce that many tanks and planes?

Or, did we build Roosevelt's Arsenal for Democracy and grow our economy even further by providing our returning heroes with a chance to go to college and own their own home?

Again, we chose to act, and again, we rose together.

Today, at the beginning of this young century, we have to decide again. But this time, it's your turn to choose.

Here in Galesburg, you know what this new challenge is. You've seen it.

You see it when you drive by the old Maytag plant around lunchtime and no one walks out anymore. I saw it during the campaign when I met the union guys who used to work at the plant and now wonder what they're gonna do at 55-years-old without a pension or health care; when I met the man whose son needs a new liver but doesn't know if he can afford it when the kid gets to the top of the transplant list.

It's as if someone changed the rules in the middle of the game and no one bothered to tell these people. And, in reality, the rules have changed.

It started with technology and automation that rendered entire occupations obsolete—when was the last time anybody here stood in line for the bank teller instead of going to the ATM, or talked to a switchboard operator? Then companies like Maytag were able to pick up and move their factories to some Third World country where workers are a lot cheaper than they are in the U.S.

As Tom Friedman points out in his new book, *The World Is Flat,* over the last decade or so, these forces—technology and globalization—have combined like never before. So that while most of us have been paying attention to how much easier technology has made our lives—sending e-mails on BlackBerries, surfing the Web on our cell phones, instant messaging with friends across the world—a quiet revolution has been breaking down barriers and connecting the world's economies. Now, businesses not only have the ability to move jobs wherever there's a factory, but wherever there's an internet connection.

Countries like India and China realized this. They understood that they need not be just a source of cheap labor or cheap exports. They can compete with us on a global scale. The one resource they still needed was a skilled, educated labor force. So they started schooling their kids earlier, longer, and with a greater emphasis on math, science, and technology, until their most talented students realized they don't have to immigrate to America to have a decent life—they can stay right where they are.

The result? China is graduating four times the number of engineers that the United States is graduating. Not only are those Maytag employees competing with Chinese and Indonesian and Mexican workers, now you are too. Today, accounting firms are e-mailing your tax returns to workers in India who will figure them out and send them back as fast as any worker in Indiana could.

When you lose your luggage in a Boston airport, tracking it down may involve a call to an agent in Bangalore, who will find it by making a phone call to Baltimore. Even the Associated Press has outsourced some of their jobs to writers all over the world who can send in a story with the click of a mouse.

As British Prime Minister Tony Blair has said, in this new economy, "talent is 21st century wealth." If you've got the skills, you've got the education, and you have the opportunity to upgrade and improve both, you'll be able to compete and win anywhere. If not, the fall will be further and harder than ever before.

So what do we do about this? How does America find our way in this new, global economy? What will our place in history be?

Like so much of the American story, once again, we face a choice. Once again, there are those who believe that there isn't much we can do about this as a nation. That the best idea is to give everyone one big refund on their government—divvy it up into individual portions, hand it out, and encourage everyone to use their share to go buy their own health care, their own retirement plan, their own child care, their own education, and so forth.

In Washington, they call this the Ownership Society. But in our past there has been another term for it—Social Darwinism, every man and woman for him or herself. It's a tempting idea, because it doesn't require much thought or ingenuity. It allows us to say to those whose health care or tuition may rise faster than they can afford—tough luck. It allows us to say to the Maytag workers who have lost their job—life isn't fair. It lets us say to the child who was born into poverty—pull yourself up by your bootstraps. And it is especially tempting because each of us believes we will always be the winner in life's lottery, that we will be Donald Trump, or at least that we won't be the chump that he tells: "You're fired!"

But there is a problem. It won't work. It ignores our history. It ignores the fact that it has been government research and investment that made the railways and the internet possible. It has been the creation of a massive middle class, through decent wages and benefits and public schools— that has allowed all of us to prosper. Our economic dominance has depended on individual initiative and belief in the free market; but it has also has depended on our sense of mutual regard for each other, the idea that everybody has a stake in the country, that we're all in it together and everybody's got a shot at opportunity—that has produced our unrivaled political stability.

And so if we do nothing in the face of globalization, more people will continue to lose their health care. Fewer kids will be able to afford the diploma you're about to receive.

More companies like United won't be able to provide pensions for their employees. And those Maytag workers will be joined in the unemployment line by any worker whose skill can be bought and sold on the global market.

Today I'm here to tell you what most of you already know. This isn't us. This isn't how our story ends—not in this country. America is a land of big dreamers and big hopes.

It is this hope that has sustained us through revolution and civil war, depression and world war, a struggle for civil and social rights and the brink of nuclear crisis. And it is because of our dreamers that we have emerged from each challenge more united, more prosperous, and more admired than ever before.

So let's dream. Instead of doing nothing or simply defending 20th century solutions, let's imagine together what we can do to give every American a fighting chance in the 21st century.

What if we prepared every child in America with the education and skills they need to compete in this new economy? If we made sure college was affordable for everyone who wanted to go? If we walked up to those Maytag workers and told them that their old job wasn't coming back, but that the new jobs will be there because of the serious job re-training and lifelong education that is waiting for them—the sorts of opportunities that Knox has created with the Strong Futures scholarship program?

What if no matter where you worked or how many times you switched jobs, you had health care and a pension that stayed with you always, so that each of us had the flexibility to move to a better job or start a new business?

And what if instead of cutting budgets for research and development and science, we fueled the genius and the innovation that will lead to the new jobs and new industries of the future?

Right now, all across America, there are amazing discoveries being made. If we supported these discoveries on a national level, if we committed ourselves to investing in these possibilities, just imagine what it could do for a town like Galesburg. Ten or twenty years down the road, that old Maytag plant could re-open its doors as an Ethanol refinery that turns corn into fuel.

Down the street, a biotechnology research lab could open that's on the cusp of discovering a cure for cancer. And across the way, a new auto company could be busy churning out electric cars. The new jobs created would be filled by American workers trained with new skills and a world-class education. None of this will come easy. Every one of us will have to work more, read more, train more, think more. We will have to slough off bad habits—like driving gas guzzlers that weaken our economy and feed our enemies abroad. Our kids will have to turn off the TV sets and put away the video games and start hitting the books. We will have to reform institutions, like our public schools, that were designed for an earlier time. Republicans will have to recognize our collective responsibilities, even as Democrats recognize that we have to do more than just defend the old programs.

It won't be easy, but it can be done. It can be our future. We have the talent and the resources and the brainpower. But now we need the political will. We need a national commitment.

And we need you.

Now, no one can force you to meet these challenges. If you want, it will be pretty easy for you to leave here today and not give another thought to towns like Galesburg and the challenges they face. There is no community service requirement in the real world; no one's forcing you to care. You can take your diploma, walk off this stage, and go chasing after the big house, and the nice suits, and all the other things that our money culture says you can buy.

But I hope you don't. Focusing your life solely on making a buck shows a poverty of ambition. It asks too little of yourself. You need to take up the challenges that we face as a nation and make them your own.

Not because you have a debt to all of those who helped you get where you are, although you do have that debt. Not because you have an obligation to those who are less fortunate, although you do have that obligation. You need to take on the challenge because you have an obligation to yourself. Because our individual salvation depends on collective salvation. Because it's only when you hitch your wagon to something larger than yourself that you will realize your true potential. And if we're willing to share the risks and the rewards this new century offers, it will be a victory for each of you, and for every American.

You're wondering how you'll do this. The challenges are so big. And it seems so difficult for one person to make a difference.

But we know it can be done. Because where you're sitting, in this very place, in this town, it's happened before.

Nearly two centuries ago, before civil rights and voting rights, before Abraham Lincoln and the Civil War, before all of that, America was stained with the sin of slavery. In the sweltering heat of southern plantations, men and women who looked like me would dream of the day they could escape the life of pain and servitude into which they were sold like cattle. And yet, year after year, as this moral cancer ate away at the American ideals of liberty and equality, the nation was silent.

But its people would not stay silent for long.

One by one, abolitionists emerged to tell their fellow Americans that this would not be our place in history. That this was not the America that had captured the imagination of so many around the world.

The resistance they met was fierce, and some paid with their lives. But they would not be deterred, and they soon spread out across the country to fight for their cause. One man from New York went west, all the way to the prairies of Illinois to start a colony.

And here in Galesburg, freedom found a home.

Here in Galesburg, the main depot for the Underground Railroad in Illinois, escaped slaves could freely roam the streets and take shelter in people's homes. And when their masters or the police would come for them, the people of this town would help them escape north, some literally carrying them in their arms.

Think about the risks that involved—if they were caught abetting these fugitives, they could have been jailed or lynched. It would have been so easy for these simple townspeople to just turn the other way; to go on living their lives in a private peace.

And yet, they carried them. Why?

Perhaps it is because they knew that they were all Americans; that they were all brothers and sisters; and in the end, their own salvation would be forever linked to the salvation of this land they called home.

The same reason that a century later, young men and women your age would take a Freedom Ride down south, to work for the Civil Rights movement. The same reason that black women across the South chose to walk instead of ride the bus after a long day of doing other people's laundry, cleaning other people's kitchens.

Today, on this day of possibility, we stand in the shadow of a lanky, raw-boned man with little formal education who once took the stage at Old Main and told the nation that if anyone did not believe the American principles of freedom and equality were timeless and all-inclusive, they should go rip that page out of the Declaration of Independence.

My hope for all of you is that you leave here today with the will to keep these principles alive in your own life and the life of this country. They will be tested by the challenges of this new century, and at times we may fail to live up to them. But know that you have it within your power to try. That generations who have come before you faced these same fears and uncertainties in their own time. And that through our labor, and through God's providence, and our willingness to shoulder each other's burdens, America will continue on its precious journey towards that distant horizon, and a better day.

Thank you, and congratulations on your graduation.